INSECURE

Overcome Jealousy, Fear Of Abandonment and Anxiety. Healing Your Anxious Attachment Wounds And Save Your Codependent Relationship.

by

Edward Miles

© **Copyright 2020 by *Edward Miles.***

All rights reserved.

This document is geared towards providing exact and reliable information with regards to the topic and issue covered. The publication is sold with the idea that the publisher is not required to render accounting, officially permitted, or otherwise, qualified services. If advice is necessary, legal or professional, a practiced individual in the profession should be ordered.

From a Declaration of Principles which was accepted and approved equally by a Committee of the American Bar Association and a Committee of Publishers and Associations.

In no way is it legal to reproduce, duplicate, or transmit any part of this document in either electronic means or in printed format. Recording of this publication is strictly prohibited and any storage of this document is not allowed unless with written permission from the publisher. All rights reserved.

The information provided herein is stated to be truthful and consistent, in that any liability, in terms of inattention or otherwise, by any usage or abuse of any policies, processes, or directions contained within is the solitary and utter responsibility of the recipient reader. Under no circumstances will any legal responsibility or blame be held against the publisher for any reparation, damages, or monetary loss due to the information herein, either directly or indirectly.

Respective authors own all copyrights not held by the publisher.

The information herein is offered for informational purposes solely, and is universal as so. The presentation of the information is without contract or any type of guarantee assurance.

The trademarks that are used are without any consent, and the publication of the trademark is without permission or backing by the trademark owner. All trademarks and brands within this book are for clarifying purposes only and are the owned by the owners themselves, not affiliated with this document

TABLE OF CONTENTS

INTRODUCTION 7

CHAPTER ONE: A FOUNDATION OF LOVE 14

   THE BASICS OF HOW YOU CONNECT 17

   ATTACHMENT RELATED ANXIETY 19

   FOUR STYLES OF ATTACHMENT 20

      Secure Attachment: Happy in Love 25

      Preoccupied Attachment: Desperate for Love 26

      Dismissing Attachment: No Need for Love 29

      Fearful Attachment: Conflicted in Love 33

   FINDING YOUR ATTACHMENT STYLE 35

CHAPTER TWO: WHY YOU RELATE THE WAY YOU DO 40

   CLOSENESS: PROTECTION FROM DANGER 41

   PLACE OF REFUGE: THE NEED FOR COMFORT 42

   SECURE BASE: SUPPORT TO EXPLORE THE WORLD 45

      Adjusting Autonomy and Closeness 47

   PREOCCUPIED: GRASPING FOR CLOSENESS 48

   DISMISSING: MAKING IT ALL ALONE 49

   FEARFUL: LOST IN RELATIONSHIPS 51

   DEALING WITH YOUR EMOTIONS 54

      Anxiety and Overwhelmed 55

Feelings? What Emotions? 60

THE CHEMISTRY OF "SECURE AND HAPPY" 61

TWO WAYS TO EARN SECURITY AND HAPPY RELATIONSHIPS 64

CHAPTER THREE: OPEN YOURSELF TO CHANGE 68

FIGURING OUT HOW TO SEE YOURSELF IN A POSITIVE LIGHT 72

Affirming the "You" You Know 73

Challenging Selective Attention 75

Challenging Selective Memory 76

Challenging Selective Interpretation 76

AFFIRMING HOW YOU SEE OTHERS 77

CLOSED LOOP RELATIONSHIPS 79

INTEREST WITHDRAWAL: A COMMON RELATIONSHIP PROBLEM 82

SURVEY YOUR PATTERNS 88

SUMMARY: GAINING PERSPECTIVE 89

CHAPTER FOUR: DEALING WITH OBSTACLES 91

SELF-DECEPTION 92

THE LOGIC STOPS HERE 96

HOW PAIN MOTIVATES CHANGE 102

THE NEED FOR NEW EXPERIENCES 104

CHAPTER FIVE: LASTING SECURITY PATH 109

AWARENESS 112

FAMILIARITY WITH EMOTIONS 113

5

RECOGNIZING THOUGHTS AND EMOTIONS *117*

ATTENTION TO THOUGHTS... *120*

MENTALIZING... *122*

SELF-COMPASSION.. *125*

SELF-KINDNESS *126*

BASIC HUMANITY... *128*

MINDFULNESS... *128*

ADVANTAGES OF SELF-COMPASSION *132*

THE HEALING POWER OF COMPASSIONATE SELF-AWARENESS................... *135*

CHAPTER SIX: HOW TO DEVELOP SELF-AWARENESS 142

CONFRONTING YOUR AMBIVALENCE... *143*

SUSTAINING AWARENESS OF EMOTIONS *146*

ENDURING YOUR EMOTIONS.. *151*

CHANGING YOUR THOUGHTS WITH GREATER AWARENESS........................ *153*

MENTALIZING... *159*

Introduction

Regardless of whether single or in a relationship, numerous individuals accept that they'll never be glad in affection. They feel neglected and need friendship—not only a pal to sit close to at a movie, yet a friend, associate, and darling to go with them through that most prominent of all experiences we call life. They frequently fear that their partners will jolt once they become more acquainted with "the genuine me." Sometimes, they feel that their partners welcome the things they do. However, this isn't enough. Well, try to imagine a scenario in which their exposition hesitates. Then there's the ever-present worry of whether anybody would really be there for them if they let themselves be helpless by seeking that individual for help, solace, and consolation. In case you identify with any of these battles, then this book is the right one for you.

You might be prepared with loads of information, some advice from experts, or a "demonstrated recipe" for a successful relationship. It might originate from loved ones, self-improvement guides and articles, or even from your advisor. You may have attempted to meet Mr. or then again Ms.

Directly by mingling more, dating consistently, or sharpening your online profile. In case you're as of now in relationship, may have rehearsed self-assuredness and successful relational abilities, just as advising yourself that you are deserving of affection. However, at the same time, you battle with feeling desolate and unlovable, or constantly fearing dismissal. There is a purpose behind this; and there is also an answer.

As with nearly everything else throughout everyday life, you find out about attachment ships through understanding. Furthermore, since your first genuine relationship started as a baby with your guardians, that is the place you started finding out about relationships. I realize that is one of the adages of brain science, but at the same time it's actual. Your first exercises on how accessible and sustaining others will be the point at which you need them, and on how adorable yourself are, depended on the glow, acknowledgment, and consolation offered by your folks or other people who dealt with you. During the early months and long stretches of your life, you built up a specific style of associating with—and joining to—other people.

Despite the fact that you might not have known about this style until either immaturity or adulthood (or perhaps it's as yet muddled), your present style is most likely on a very basic level equivalent to what was supported in youth. In case your initial encounters left you doubting your feeling of being deserving of affection, frightful of being dismissed, or with an insatiable hunger for consolation, then you most likely despite everything feel thusly. It could likewise be that complicated encounters further down the road increased anxiety about relationships that recently hidden under the surface. In any case, the essential weakness to this attachment related to anxiety was, most likely, created during youth.

Understand that attachment related anxiety doesn't need to be in light of any clearly damaging or destructive child rearing; indeed, it frequently isn't. Several individuals with attachment related anxiety originate from loving homes. Shockingly, their folks' own battles, difficult or horrendous conditions meddled with them having the option to parent viably, at least, when they genuinely loved their kids.

You may ponder, can my attachment related anxiety tenaciously remain with me through life? In order to answer this, consider the basically unbounded number of communications you had with your folks or different guardians during your adolescence, for a long time, after a seemingly endless amount of time. (Truly,

9

Moving toward your relationship battles from this point of view is exactly the topic that this book is about.

Insecure in Love clarifies, in a quite straightforward language, how your relationship battles previously framed; shouldn't something be said about this procedure makes change so hard; and how those troubles can be survived with the goal that you can enjoy a protected, enduring affection.

While the primary purpose of this book is to enable you to understand what you can do to discover joy in a close attachment, the thoughts that I will present can likewise assist you with understanding your partner better.

In some cases a window into your partner's reality is actually what you have to identify with that person more mercifully, which thusly can assist you with nurturing a more beneficial relationship.

Chapter One: A Foundation Of Love

To see a birth is to observe a marvel. No mother can oppose to hold, nestle with, and keep an eye on her infant. Also, this is the place the tale of each individual's existence of relationships and love starts.

Newborn children truly need their parental figures for survival. This way, because of Mother Nature, newborn children are patterned with a need to connect with others, and the fortitude to do it. For example, they like to see individuals' countenances, can get others to think about them by crying, and are typically console by being either held or shaken. Also, obviously, coddles simply look so darned charming that individuals need to think about them. All this keeps their essential parental figures (as a rule their moms, and optionally their dads) keen on ensuring and supporting them. As kids become versatile, their proceeded with requirement for help to endure persuades them to stay nearby to their moms. A little one who adventures out will definitely think back to Mommy for consolation.

It's during these early years, starting with earliest stages that individuals initially figure out how relationships can assist them with having a sense of security and can quiet them when they are vexed.

Any individual who's had involvement in infants and little children has watched these practices, yet psychoanalyst John Bowlby started to distribute thoughts in the late 1950s about them as indications of an attachment system. He clarified that they are intended to keep a "more grounded and additionally more astute" individual—an attachment figure—close with the goal that the kid can endure and have a sense of security. He additionally offered the progressive thought that with the end goal for kids to flourish, their attachment figures should struggle warm and genuinely accessible (Bowlby, 1961, 1989). This thought was in direct clash with what moms were instructed around back in those days. The common shrewdness was that a delicate, sustaining way to deal with childrearing would make children both tenacious and excessively needy. Rather, moms were urged to keep a target, normal separation, at least, when their children were disturbed or sick (Johnson, 2008).

Bowlby's thoughts were commonly dismissed until scientist Mary Ainsworth helped him to demonstrate fact of his hypotheses through her work during the 1970s, as Wallin (2007) and Mikulincer and Shaver (2007) note. Ainsworth's investigations helped showing that through countless communications with their folks—unpretentious or not all that inconspicuous—children were able to build up a method of holding that saturates their very being. Thusly of holding turns into a working model that sets their desires for how others will react to them, just as for how they feel about them-selves. Sometime later, scientists indicated that the attachment procedure was dynamic in romantic love.

While nature gives the attachment system as an approach to guarantee the kid's survival, attachment bonds created inside that system are felt as love—in both youth and adulthood. So it's nothing unexpected that children look for the love of their folks as though their lives rely upon it (which they actually do). Grown-ups experience comparative serious anxiety and difficult pity when the presence of their essential relationships (and the love those relationships offer) feels undermined.

Additionally, is not to be considered unexpected that children who will in general get resentful effectively and experience difficulty being relieved by their folks, will likewise battle with being vexed effectively as grown-ups, and can't locate a steady, solid feeling of calming and wellbeing in their romantic relationships.

The Basics of How You Connect

Whom do you go to whenever you are truly disturbed? At those occasions, your attachment system is turned on; like turning on an inner homing gadget for which the objective or "home" is an attachment figure. When a grown-up's system functions admirably, he has a protected style of attachment. He searches out his partner or any other essential attachment figure for consolation in case he's disturbed. And, when he sees her as dependably accessible and adequately responsive, his attachment system kills. He feels quiet and supported. In any case, individuals with an insecure example of attachment don't completely or reliably find such solace in their partners or in others, a sign that their "homing gadget" is failing.

Momentum research (Bartholomew and Horowitz, 1991) recommends that attachment styles (regardless of whether secure or insecure) are in a general sense dependent on two basic "working models" (or default methods of relating)— these are a working model of self and a working model of others.

The working model of self is your feeling of how commendable or dishonorable you feel of being cherished. As you would imagine, whenever you feel shameful of love, you likewise fear being dismissed and battle with attachment related anxiety. You may perceive this as anxiety—a feeling of anxiety or anxiety. Yet, you could likewise feel it as some other troubling feelings, for example, misery, forlornness, or outrage as well. Grown-ups and kids with a solid feeling of disgracefulness live as if their attachment system, or homing gadget for an attachment figure, is stuck in the completely "on" position. If you relate to this, you might be continually looking for consolation from an attachment figure and constantly feel alone, dismissed, or in fear of rejection. Furthermore, even at the less outrageous degrees of attachment related anxiety, individuals can battle with feeling to some insufficient degree, and fear of not being able to feel partner handle rejection.

This book is intended to assist you with defeating such misery, whatever your degree of attachment related anxiety is.

Additionally, individuals have a working model of others—a desire for whether others will be sincerely accessible to them. To the degree that they expect that others won't be there for them, they feel awkward with drawing near and need to avoid from it. This is the thing that therapists define as attachment related shirking. There are a few people who are certain to the point that others won't be sincerely accessible that they choose struggles completely confident. They do everything they can to attempt to keep them-selves from wanting to rely upon another person. Maybe their attachment system or homing gadget is stuck in the "off" position.

Exercise: How Much Anxiety and Avoidance Do You Feel in Your Relationships?

In order to figure out how much attachment related anxiety and attachment related shirking you experience, think about how well you fit the passages beneath. Rate yourself on a size of 0–10, with 0 being not in any manner and 10 being that you totally relate.

Clutch these numbers with the goal that you can use them later while evaluating your attachment style.

Attachment Related Anxiety

Being absolutely sincerely close with my partner means the world to me. Yet, others would prefer not struggles as close as I might want struggles, and my longing struggles so close frequently frightens them off. When I have an partner, I question myself and I become worried that I'm not equivalent to him or others. I'm constantly stressed that he couldn't mindfulness less over me as much as I mindfulness about him. Furthermore, I likewise stress constantly over whether my partner truly loves me, will stop loving me, or even worse will choose to leave me.

I'm particularly stressed that he'll see another person when we are not together.

Rating:

Attachment Related Avoidance

I am a free, independent individual, so I should be in a nearby, serious relationship. When I am in such a relationship, I lean toward not to rely upon my partner or to share deeply close to home attentions and emotions.

And, it makes me awkward when my partner needs to rely upon me or to jabber about his attentions and feelings. Whenever I run into issues, I will in general stay quiet about them and make sense of them all alone, and I'd lean toward it if my partner would do the same thing.

Rating:

Four Styles of Attachment

As I've clarified earlier, attachment styles can best be understood by joining how individuals identify with themselves (which can make anxiety) and to other people (which can bring about evasion). By separating the components of anxiety and shirking into high and low, the accompanying four potential mixes are made (see figure 1):

Preoccupied: High Anxiety, Low Avoidance Fearful:

High Anxiety, High Avoidance Dismissing:

Low Anxiety, High Avoidance Secure:

Low Anxiety, Low Avoidance

The first exploration in attachment hypothesis marked the attachment styles as being completely not stope the same as one another—similarly as a lady and a fish are completely extraordinary, except if you are given to putting stock in mermaids. Anyway, ebb and flow research (Griffin and Bartholomew, 1994) shows that this basically isn't too accurate. Rather, extraordinary attachment styles speak to "foggy" bunches that uncover propensities, however should not be taken too serious.

Consolidating levels of shirking and anxiety works just like mixing two essential hues. Red and yellow make orange. However, adding only somewhat yellow to red makes an orangey-red; and adding only somewhat red to yellow makes an orangey-yellow. A comparable dynamic happens with the two elements of attachment. Think about Ann, who is high in anxiety and extremely low in shirking, and Dan, who is likewise high in anxiety yet only somewhat low in evasion.

Along a comparable line of reasoning, you might have a place more in the dismissing or secure class of attachment, yet be closer to the anxiety end of that gathering. Well, this is how you will identify: with a significant number of the battles of tensely joined individuals without really being unmistakably restlessly connected. Therefore, you will likewise profit by reading futher.

By understanding the "haziness" of these groupings, you will have the option to use this book more successfully. It is enticing to survey your style of attachment and afterward categorize yourself. For instance, you may think about yourself having a preoccupied or frightful attachment style. In any case, you would not be taking all parts of you—the extraordinary individual that you are—into account. The most ideal approach in order to diminish your relationship anxiety and develop yourself depends to a great extent on self-understanding. So when you read about the four attachment styles, think about the amount you identify with everyone and not simply which class you fit in.

It's additionally imperative to perceive that your attachment style can change with understanding. For example, think about Heather. She had consistently felt deficient as an individual, and showed a quite preoccupied attachment style. Her better half, Alan, strengthened this inclination with his successive spotlight on her missteps and deficiencies. He, in the long run, divided from her, leaving her to battle considerably more with a more deep feeling of being unlovable. However, with treatment she started genuinely scrutinizing this negative perspective on herself.

For example, she had the option to understand that Alan had been excessively basic. Then she met Sam, who esteemed both her awareness and imagination. She relaxed in his love and warmth, which softened her staying self-rejection and helped her to feel increasingly good with being esteemed by another individual. Romantic relationships regularly fill in as an uncommon open door for you to update your attachment style—an open door that this book can assist you with.

Notwithstanding surveying your own style of attachment, think about different styles, as well. Think about the styles of your current or past partners, or even your friends and partners. Your attachment related anxiety can incite you to make speedy, and frequently wrong, emotional decisions of others. Accordingly, you may misconstrue your partner's feelings, battles as well as practices. This can cause critical issues within your relationship. By understanding your partner's attachment style better, you can get him and the elements among you better. Additionally, by having a good handle of secure attachment, you are able to understand the advantages of moving in the direction of this for yourself and you can see how having a safely joined partner can support you.

One final significant specification before you read about the attachment styles: A straightforward reading of these styles will, most likely, leave you with the feeling that the main "great" approach to have a healthy relationship is to have a protected attachment style. This impression would not be right. The "best" approach to join is to have a romantic relationship that satisfies you. If you incline toward having a preoccupied style of attachment and are hitched to somebody who has that inclination as well, however you two are upbeat—then trust in that. Enjoy it. Your style and life condition are directly for you. As it occurs, one critical way (however not by any means the only method) of finding bliss in your relationship when you are despondent, is to keep pushing towards an increasingly secure style. However, as you evaluate your life and what you should transform, it is significant for you to watch out for the genuine "prize": satisfaction in love.

Secure Attachment: Happy in Love

Sue is essentially an upbeat individual. She loves her work as a grade teacher and thinks that she is excellent at it. In her off hours she enjoys playing tennis and climbing with two of her nearby young lady friends.

She is additionally joyfully connected with to Keith, whom she unhesitatingly trusts and depends on for help. Obviously, no relationship is great. For example, there was the point at which he stood her up for supper since he disregarded their deals: in the eternal expressions of Ricky Ricardo, he had "loads of 'splainin' to do." But even in such a situation, when she blows up with him, they can talk through their issues and she winds up feeling that he truly cares about her.

Like around 60% of individuals, Sue is safely connected. Safely appended people are fundamentally alright with their full scope of feelings and feel like adorable, great and mindful. They are likewise disposed to think about their partners as dependable, good natured, touchy, and genuinely there for them. So they are content both with themselves and in their relationships.

Similarly as they are alright with their relationships when is all said and done, safely appended individuals are likewise content with their sexual experiences. Setting a high need on emotional closeness, they will generally stay dedicated, feel good talking about sex, and appreciate the joys that it brings to the table.

If you are restlessly appended and lucky enough to have a safely joined partner, then you will locate this steady and positive method of identifying to be consoling, giving you a chance to build up a more secure attachment style.

Preoccupied Attachment: Desperate for Love

Meet Rachel—somebody you may identify yourself with. She looks to her beau, Phil, to promise her that she is deserving of love since she is uncertain about this. Yet, when he is friendly and shows enthusiasm for her, she doesn't have the foggiest idea what to think since it doesn't fit at all with her self-observations. She continually stresses over the amount Phil truly thinks about her. She's certain that once he becomes more acquainted with "the genuine me," he'll promptly leave her. Therefore, she continually stresses out that he won't have any desire to get along with her during the weekends. Additionally, at whatever point he doesn't react quickly to her writings, she accepts that he's staying away from her. This chance of rejection is overpowering, thus she is worried with that fear.

Individuals like Rachel, who clearly have a preoccupied attachment style are delicate to the chance of being ignored or dismissed by their partner, whom they have to secure them. So, they use hyperactivating procedures in order to keep their attachment system "turned on" (or actuated), which guarantees that they will keep on searching out a solid attachment figure. For example, they frequently go overboard to issues and under-gauge their ability to adapt; they might as well continually examine for potential issues before, in the present, and in the future. While making these negative feelings and thoughts, they increase their requirement for an attachment figure and are basically shouting out for one. Lamentably, the individuals who do this to an outrageous can likewise wind up feeling incessantly overpowered, defenseless, and penniless as well.

Their affectability to any potential indications of rejection inadvertently prompts battles and makes separation in their personal relationships.

It's certainly a given that eventually their partners will misjudge them, be truly inaccessible, or not react in a mindful way; however, individuals with preoccupied attachment styles will see this with caution.

An away form of this is the manner by how upset Rachel becomes when Phil doesn't promptly react to her writings. Even though individuals with a preoccupied style may start a relationship feeling inebriated by their new love, they regularly become involved with their own misery very quickly. Then they are able to think about their struggles as heartless (or not reliably accessible), conniving, and perhaps unfaithful. This prompts them being possessive and ridiculously envious. To exacerbate the situation, they are frequently unfit to quiet down enough to excuse their partners for any bad behavior. So their relationships are precarious and effectively disturbed by constant issues. Therefore, individuals like Rachel are typically troubled in love. Since their attachment needs and battles feel so solid, several people with a preoccupied attachment style sort out their lives around attempting to demonstrate that they are deserving of love, or attempting to occupy them-selves from their antagonistic emotions. This meddles with their ability to communicate in a real manner. Rachel, for instance, did very well in school, yet made due with a vocation as an assistant after graduation—and stayed in it for a considerable amount of time—since she was unable to choose how to manage her four year certification in English.

Additionally, she was constantly stressed at work over what others thought of her exhibition. Even though it didn't go very far with Rachel, individuals with a preoccupied style frequently convey their issues and misery from home into work. Also, the consistent anxiety that they feel frequently messes wellbeing up.

Similarly as they do with the rest of their lives, individuals with a preoccupied attachment style approach their sexual experiences with a drive to pick up consolation and avoid rejection. So, even though they frequently enjoy being held and stroked without truly needing more sexual closeness, they go to sex to get the confirmation and acknowledgment that they are looking for. Men, in their efforts to feel cherished and acknowledged by a lady, will in general be more explicitly held to search for their partner struggles explicitly responsive and satisfied. On the other hand, ladies, in their efforts to feel loved and acknowledged by a man, will generally be less held, or once in a while unbridled. In both cases, they regularly battle with feeling that their partners or situations control their sexual experiences, and they are frequently awkward chatting with their partners about sex.

Dismissing Attachment: No Need for Love

As an example, meet Andy. Think about whether you identify with him by any means, or whether he seems like anybody you know. He is glad for his autonomy, his independence, and his promise to his business work. He is delighted in investing energy with his ex, Chris, however he wasn't too disturbed when she cut off their association. To him, she made a big deal of his excursions for work by needing him to call her, however she just requested an infrequent registration. He likewise felt she needed to discuss her emotions and their relationship "constantly." So now he's glad about not dealing with her anymore. Even though he, in some cases, learns about being left aside when his friends are discussing their lady friends, he says he's not troubled by it and really wants to spend time alone by humself.

What Andy denies, even to himself, is that he effectively limits and keeps away from his feelings. This is exceptionally normal for individuals with a dismissing attachment style, and it places them in danger for both anxiety and sadness.

Like the ones with a preoccupied style, those with a dismissing style are likewise inclined to accept that their partners won't dependably be there to help or solace them. In any case, they ensure themselves by unknowingly using deactivating procedures that "turn off" (or deactivate) their attachment system, thus empowering them to abstain from being in the illogical situation of feeling a draw to depend on an undependable partner. They successfully restrain, avoid from, or overlook their feelings as well as attachment needs. They will in general stay far off, limit their communications and inti-mate discussions, and regularly slander their partners. For instance, while Andy regularly appeared struggling caring as he helped Chris with her funds, which she increased in value, this likewise permitted him to stay in a far off and unrivaled position, which just expanded her negative emotions about herself. During different occasions, Andy would keep a protected separation and react to Chris' efforts struggles genuinely personal by disclosing to her that she was "simply excessively poor." This, obviously, just expanded her self-questions. Finally, dismissing individuals may genuinely think about their partners, however they do as such without getting either excessively cozy or sincerely trapped.

For the most part ignorant of their feelings, dismissing individuals aren't completely outfitted to adapt to sincerely upsetting encounters.

For instance, when their partners disturb them, they attempt to either limit or deny their resentment. In any case, that outrage keeps on existing under the surface, frequently making them both tense and unforgiving. This dynamic, obviously, doesn't look good for their relationships; however it can't be effortlessly tended to or redressed because such an extensive amount it happens outside their awareness. This dynamic is generally risky for restlessly joined partners, who will in general decipher the dismissing partner's resentment as proof that there is some kind of setback with them.

So why doesn't the dismissing partner simply leave? Indeed, even those with a dismissing style need both solace and association. So they search out and stay in romantic relationships, even as they at the same time secure themselves by being unnecessarily independent in those relationships.

Dismissing individuals approach their sexualities in the equivalent far off and self-defensive route as they take part in relationship all in all.

Since physical or sexual contact can debilitate their safeguards, many are awkward with connecting through touch, for instance, with either embraces or delicate stroking. They may go without sex, sometimes deciding to depend on masturbation. Or on the other hand they may stay sincerely removed by restricting sex to single night rendezvous or momentary relationships that are just cursorily close. When they are in personal relationships, they tend not struggles friendly and might be genuinely withdrawn during sex. This can leave anxiety partners feeling ugly as well as dishonorable of love.

Fearful Attachment: Conflicted in Love

John depicts himself as an emotional chaos. He has been like this since he was a child. By the age of fourteen, he was basically dealing with himself since his dad was a furious smashed and his mom was caught up with attempting to hold the family together while working extended periods of time. He thinks about himself imperfect, destitute, powerless, and shameful of love as well. Also, he accepts that others realize something isn't right with him and therefore stay away.

So even though he would adore a submitted, romantic relationship, he abstains from drawing near out of fear that he'll be dismissed or misconstrued.

This contention between an extraordinary fear of rejection and an urgent requirement for consolation and closeness is a run of the mill of individuals with a frightful attachment style. When they are not absolutely maintaining a strategic distance from relationships, they wind up carrying on in opposing and confusing ways. Inclined to think about partners to be sincerely removed, they generally urgently attempt to stand out enough to be noticed by using hyperactivating techniques, for example, misrepresenting their trouble. However, when they see their partners as drawing near, they feel powerless against getting injured. Therefore, they naturally hope to shield themselves from their partner, going to deactivating methodologies to avoid from closeness. In case of John's situation, he would go through his ends of the week fixing old furnishings, constraining the time he could be with his better half (when he had one). This steady strain between being either excessively close or too far off leaves frightfully connected individuals incessantly bothered, insecure, very inactive, and genuinely inaccessible too.

As anyone might expect, they are at high risk for anxiety, wretchedness, and some other emotional battles.

Persuaded that their partners are relationally stunted, individuals completely connected with fear, will in general view their partners in an especially negative light as well as experience difficulty understanding them. For example, when John was dating Amanda and would meet her after work for supper, he would perpetually finish up being uninterested in her when she was extremely simply tired from a taxing day. This inclination, obviously, causes anxiety in relationship. In any case, those with a frightful style are probably going to simply stew in their feelings instead of legitimately address them. Presumably in light of their feeling that they are disgraceful of love, they will generally stay in their relationships at least, whenever those companionships are genuinely disturbed or even damaging. Then again, due to their inconvenience with closeness and being valued (which is what they frantically need), they are probably going to feel something isn't right and cut off an association, at least, when they are captivated and their partner is genuinely mindful.

Similarly as they battle with being sincerely private with their partners, they additionally battle with being genuinely cozy. Every now and then, this implies using easygoing sex as a method of outstanding sincerely removed and safe while likewise attempting to address their issue for solace, acknowledgment, and consolation as well. They may do this with either single night rendezvous or transient relationships (that end when they begin feeling powerless). When they are less focused on meeting their attachment needs and are more in the method of ensuring themselves, they are, most likely, going to evade sexual closeness and it's going with powerlessness.

Finding Your Attachment Style

If you have not effectively done as such, audit the four styles of attachment and choose which one you best identify yourself with.

However, recall, you are probably not going to fit any of the styles perfectly. So focus on how your own attachment style fuses a portion of the attributes of some different styles. For example, would you say you are essentially secure yet with a habit toward questioning your self-esteem (being preoccupied)?

Likewise remember that, even though you have a specific, trademark style, it will probably change a piece with several relationships.

Another way you can survey your style of attachment is to chart your evaluations on the elements of anxiety and shirking. You should get a spotless piece of paper. (Diagram paper is ideal, if you have it.) Draw a flat line and mark it Anxiety. Spot uniformly divided spasm marks along it, numbering them from 0 to 10 (from left to right). Then, at the 5, draw a vertical line and mark it as Avoidance. Once more, place uniformly divided spasm marks along it and number them from 0 to 10 (from base to top, setting the 5 where this line crosses the flat line). Make sure you duplicate the style portrayals from think about 1 along with every one of the quadrants on your chart. In order to decide your rating for attachment related anxiety and attachment related shirking, think back to the exercise "The amount Anxiety and Avoidance Do You Feel in Your Relationships?" Using your two evaluations, plot where you fall in the quadrants and spot a speck there. You will not only see the style quadrant into which you fall, however, you will likewise perceive that you are so near to every one of different quadrants.

The less outrageous you are on every one of the measurements, the less your attributes will coordinate the prototypical style of the quadrant that you are in.

A third method to decide your attachment style in personal relationships is to use an online study. Alongside uncovering your attachment style, it additionally shows where you fall on a chart of attachment related anxiety and attachment related shirking.

Once you are clear about your own attachment style, you should look at the attachment style of your partner or past partners. You can rate them in a similar way you evaluated yourself, using your perceptions about them and their practices as well. You can likewise have current partners rate themselves if they are available to it; the benefit of this is that it can open some lighting up and closeness building discussions. In the two cases, understanding their style of attachment will assist you with improving them and the relationship you two have or had. Finally, realizing your attachment style is a viable initial step to evolving it. So you've just achieved a great deal just by getting to this point. Seeing how your style created is additionally significant. Also, this is something that I'll talk about straightaway.

Chapter Two: Why You Relate The Way You Do

My objective, in this section, is to explain the advancement of attachment styles in the right way so that you can look at yourself (and your partner) and genuinely state, "Well, obviously you're battling with that. How you are thinking and feeling promise well." As with any issue, the initial move toward an answer is to approach it with an inspirational mentality as well as a genuine understanding.

To begin with, it's basic that you understand the attachment system's three essential capacities. These are:

Nearness: People normally endeavor to keep their attachment figure (typically a parent or romantic partner) close.

Place of refuge: Whenever individuals feel compromised, they look to an attachment figure for insurance, solace, and backing.

Secure base: When individuals have a sense of security and bolstered around an attachment figure, they feel a lot more liberated to seek after objectives divided from that relationship.

Your involvement with grown-up relationships is mainly identified with how well each one of these capacities was met via parental figures during your adolescence, and how well they've been met by attachment figures in ensuing relationships. No, you can't accuse it just for your folks. Yet, a solid, educated think back can go far toward making a course for healthier relationships, by explaining where you originated from.

Closeness: Protection from Danger

The security of small kids is reliant on guardians being close and mindful. Indeed, even as children develop into pre-adulthood and youthful adulthood, they depend on their folks despite everything, however the parent-kid relationship changes essentially. They widen their system of attachment figures thus may likewise depend on some other relatives, tutors, ministry, or dear friends. And afterward, essentially, they regularly look to a romantic partner (in the long run a friend) as their foremost attachment figure in order to assist them with having a sense of security and to help their inclinations.

However, "closeness" signifies something somewhat extraordinary for a grown-up than for a little child.

Grown-ups are increasingly compelling when using mental portrayals, or pictures, of attachment figures for a feeling of solace. This implies thinking about your partner, parent, or dear friend can give you the feeling that they are genuinely close, which allows you to emblematically come back to them as a place of refuge and a protected base. After quite some time, you may come to recognize such a great amount with specific parental figures that you join their method of identifying with you into yourself, thus empowering you to keep up a feeling that you have esteem and big expectations that others will be steady. Lamentably, the more you battle with attachment related anxiety, the more uncertain you are in order to really accept that you have esteem or that others respect you. Therefore, you will have more trouble using mental portrayals as a place of refuge to self-alleviate or as a safe base for investigation.

(I will come back to the possibility of mental portrayals later on in the book, since creating them is pivotal to diminishing both your anxiety and misery in relationship.)

Place of refuge: The Need for Comfort

Kids are organically wired to look to their folks as a place of refuge from dangers.

For instance, numerous small kids rush to their folks for insurance during boisterous tempests or when they meet a comedian at the carnival (which, from their point of view, is a naturally unnerving animal). However, it's insufficient for guardians to offer physical security. Children must have a sense of security and help in their folks' strength.

Guardians who can keep up their emotional harmony do the best employment of this. By not becoming involved with their own feelings, they are allowed to have sympathy for their children' encounters directly from very early stages. When children feel that their folks sympathize with and regard their encounters, they like themselves and their creating capacities. As children develop, these guardians keep on giving delicate reactions as an approach to enable them to acknowledge, understand, and adapt to their feelings as well. (Remember that no parent is whole steady or in line with her child. As opposed to being great, parental figures should just be what psychoanalyst Donald Winnicott [1953] calls "sufficient.")

Lamentably, not all guardians can do this—at least, when they love their kids. Therefore, their children don't encounter a dependable place of refuge.

They don't feel completely acknowledged, and most likely, won't feel deserving of love. They may likewise see their folks (and by expansion, others) as relationally stunted as well as unsupportive. These encounters of self as well as other people continue into adulthood. (And, as you may recollect from section 1, encounters of self and encounters of others are the two working models that underlie attachment styles). Therefore, to the degree that youth overseers were conflicting or inaccessible in furnishing you with a place of refuge, you will probably be worried with the fear of your partner leaving you; or you may very well not seek your partner for comfort.

In order to enjoy a safe and upbeat relationship, you have to confront your feelings of fear of being unlovable and dismissed, get them, and sustain another feeling of having a place of refuge in your grown-up relationships. It is anything but a simple assignment, yet it is unquestionably feasible. To assist you with confronting and understand this battle better, you should try the following exercise.

Exercise: Looking for a Safe Haven in Your Relationship

How touchy would you say you are to either physical or emotional detachments?

Whenever your partner is accomplishing something outside of your relationship, what is your opinion about it? Is it accurate to say that you are fast to feel surrendered, dismissed, or just not thought about? Provided that this is true, permit yourself to encounter, recognize, and investigate your responses (for instance, feeling painfully alone or defenseless). Recall that whatever your responses might be, they have their premise in an attachment system that was advanced to protect you from hurt. The force of your emotions is your attachment system's method of getting out, "Hello, I need assistance here! If you aren't here for me, I may pass on!"

If you are lucky enough to not feel especially delicate to detachments, think about what you do feel. How much, would you say, are you ameliorated by a feeling of your partner being with you (or by a feeling of being a piece of a couple) at least, when you are truly divided? Or then again, do you not feel enriched at least, when he is near? Think about whether you feel—or attempt to feel—divided with the goal that you are generally safe from being harmed by your partner.

Set aside some effort in order to think about situations when you and your partner have been away from one another, and carefully investigate your responses to them.

Secure Base: Support to Explore the World

Notwithstanding offering a place of refuge in a difficult situation, attachment figures additionally give kids a protected base from which they can significantly extend their experience. This is significant because individuals are brought into the world with an intrinsic "want to find out about" and ace their condition.

When kids effectively get support for this, they slowly become increasingly autonomous and thus build up a feeling of independence, an ability to act from their own inalienable advantages and qualities—for instance, a preschooler will inquisitively investigate a new den or connect with a child they don't know on the play area.

In order to build up a safe base, children need to feel cherished for what their identity is and for who they are turning out struggles. They have to find that anxieties and contrasts in enthusiasm with their folks would all be able struggles certainly worked through.

During this procedure, children likewise find that they can investigate and wander divided from their folks, and still depend on them for both help and acknowledgment.

To the degree that individuals are sufficiently blessed to have a protected base in their folks, they grow high confidence and a quite solid feeling of independence that will work well for them throughout life. They are bound to seek after their inclinations, be diligent in their efforts, and get along nicely at school and work. In their romantic relationships, they will in general feel associated with, and upheld by their partners as they surely seek after their own advantages. Moreover, they will in general enjoy solid relationships and can viably arrange social situations. In any case, this isn't the situation for everybody.

If you are involved with least a considerable lot of attachment related anxiety, reading these advantages of a safe base might feature a portion of your extraordinary battles, for example, an inability to investigate (or even distinguish) your own advantages and interests, and an aversion to communicate your-self with your partner. As hard well to feel this trouble, you're as of now taking a shot at it just by monitoring how you would profit by having a safe base. Afterwards, in parts 3 and 4 of this book, I will control you toward ways to create more prominent security inside yourself and your relationships.

Adjusting Autonomy and Closeness

To recap the past scarcely any segments: Children are inspired to stay nearby their folks, whom they see as a place of refuge. In addition, kids are inspired to investigate the world away from their folks, whom they see as a safe base. When all works out in a good way, children find that they can have both closeness and independence.

Your battles with attachment related anxiety can cloud your impression of these examples in your relationships and make it especially disappointing to understand what's turning out badly.

To help explain this, I will talk about how individuals with the diverse insecure examples of attachment balance self-rule and closeness. As you read the accompanying areas, think about how they concern you, your partner as well as your relationship.

Preoccupied: Grasping for Closeness

A few children see their folks as conflictingly accessible. It could be because the guardians are unavoidably centered around squeezing life situations or on their own emotional needs. The child's characteristic affectability is likewise a significant factor. Whatever the explanation, children who come to address whether their folks are accessible or not, are incredibly disturbed even by the idea of their folks not being there for them. This is normal for a preoccupied attachment style.

Driven by their attachment needs, such children do whatever they can in order to stand out enough struggles noticed. These fights, as John Bowlby (1961), the originator of attachment hypothesis, called them, are defined as hyperactivating system. That is, restless individuals "hyperactivate" their attachment system as their weeps for attention become more obnoxious, making them increasingly furious and regularly causing struggle within their relationships. For example, they may request that their partner help them in special manners, attempt to keep in touch, or become effectively envious and possessive.

Individuals with preoccupied attachment needs center strongly on keeping others close, to the detriment of their own advantages and now and again, even their qualities. This leaves them vacant, without an encounter of themselves that they like. Rather, they look to another person, for instance, a parent, friend, or life partner, for endorsement and direction on what interests to seek after and how to react to different conditions. Additionally, they are frequently spurred by outer, picture arranged objectives, (for example, money related riches) as an approach to get endorsement. Tragically, this quest for outer endorsement always keeps them performing, which impedes their inclination really acknowledged by an attachment figure. Along these lines, they are oftentimes left without the feeling of closeness they long for and without a positive feeling of themselves, and are unequipped to seek after their own advantages.

Dismissing: Making It all alone

While a few children are preoccupied with attempting to stand out enough struggles noticed, others stop any pretense of attempting to associate.

As Bowlby (1961) stated, after a kid's fights go more than once unanswered, or are for the most part reacted too brutally, the child encounters despair. Then, when he finally surrenders all desire for being consoled and secured, he disengages—endeavoring to deactivate his attachment system by closed-chime down his feelings and his requirement for a parental figure—and turns out struggles very confident. Then, as a grown-up, he is probably not going to encounter the closeness that accompanies romantic relationships. This portrays the dismissing style of attachment.

In case your partner inclines toward a dismissing style, you may feel con-melded when he divides himself, instead of mellowing, in light of your connecting in a strong way. The explanation behind this response is that he won't risk being let down later; so he withdraws and might turn out struggles significantly more far off. Essentially, when you are annoyed with your partner, he is probably going to show up sincerely divided and unbothered. No doubt, in any case, he certainly fears being dismissed.

Cavalier individuals miss out on two fronts. Unfit to follow up on their craving for association, they are neither really self-governing nor equipped for feeling near a partner.

Fearful: Lost in Relationships

Several children grow up with guardians who have their own solid attachment issues: they experience their folks as at times sincerely accessible, some of the time terrified, and in some cases even alarming. This variety is both confusing and alarming, and these kids can't figure out how to reliably meet their attachment needs. They don't find comfort in either deactivating (attempting to go only it) or hyperactivating (connecting for both attention and acknowledgment), so they endeavor to use the two sorts of procedures in a confused manner. This makes a disorganized and befuddling pattern in relationship known, which is known as the fearful style of attachment. In adulthood, their personal relationships are regularly loaded up with struggle and befuddling elements, as they seek both closeness and separation. As anyone might expect, they are not able to accomplish an agreeable and ameliorating feeling of closeness or a healthy feeling of self-sufficiency.

Exercise: How Well Do You Balance Autonomy and Closeness?

Obviously, relationships are a greater amount of a progressing, dynamic exercise in careful control than accomplishing some consistently held balance. In view of that, which of the accompanying pictures best speaks to your optimal relationship?

Also, which picture best speaks to your present relationship, or your latest one?

These styles are communicated in the accompanying articulations:

Secure Style:

- I am open to imparting cozy thoughts and emotions to my partner.

- I enjoy seeking after interests divided from my partner.

- I feel loved by my partner at least, whenever we seek after interests independently from one another.

- Even when we dissent, I expect that my partner will, in any case, regard and worth my feelings and me.

- I am open to rely upon my partner and having my partner rely upon me.

Anxiety Style:

- I am most agreeable when my partner and I share the whole of our thoughts, feelings as well as interests—when we appear to have converged into one.

- I am slanted to seek after what my partner enjoys, setting aside my own advantages.

- I am slanted to concede my qualities and conclusions to my partner's qualities and assessments.

- Whenever I sense my partner being far off, I feel headed to reconnect (for instance, every now and then calling or messaging); or I act irately, for example, by either pulling back or being terrible.

Avoidant Style:

- I am awkward imparting close thoughts and emotions to my partner.

- I invest heavily in acting naturally dependent enough to not require my partner.

- I am awkward relying upon my partner.

- I am awkward with my partner relying upon me.

- I enjoy seeking after interests divided from my partner.

While doing this exercise, you should draw your own covering circles and compose your own unmistakable sentences that better delineate your relationship (People are confused, so it's alright if your portrayal incorporates clashing sentences.)

Presently, think about how well your relationship addresses your issues for a:

Place of refuge: During upsetting occasions, what amount can you rely upon your partner in order to give you a feeling of solace, security as well as backing?

Secure base: How much does your partner bolster your quest for advantages and objectives divided from your relationship? How well does your relationship bolster your liking your actual feeling of what your identity is?

Dealing with Your Emotions

During outset, kids are essentially swimming in feelings. Their collaborations with their folks are unequivocally guided by their fundamental objective of endurance and they will need to have a sense of safety.

A piece of their mind called the amygdala is especially delicate to dangers to their security. It rushes to respond to potential threats, for instance, hunger, being distant from everyone else, or falling. It responds reflexively, without assessing risks and altering its response dependent on the genuine danger. When you are strolling in the forested areas and feel a surge of fear at seeing a stick that you botch as a snake, you can certainly thank your amygdala. Balancing this reaction is the ability of the hippocampus, yet that piece of the mind doesn't start to work until kids are somewhere in the range of around two and three years of age. Up to that point, all threats are seen similarly and trigger an edgy quest for a sheltered attachment figure in order to secure and relieve them. This inclination is the thing that neuroscientist Jaak Panksepp alludes to as basic frenzy (referenced in Johnson, 2008); and it keeps on being activated into adulthood at whatever point individuals feel undermined. It additionally kicks in on a regular basis when they fear losing their partner or other essential attachment figure.

Contingent upon your attachment style, you will feel base frenzy pretty much regularly; and you will be pretty much compelling in overseeing it. The exact same thing is valid for your partner, if you have one.

The aftereffect of these various encounters significantly affects your relationship. In the following three areas, I explain about how the anxiety, avoidant, and secure attachment styles influence individuals' emotional encounters and how they deal with those encounters.

Anxiety and Overwhelmed

When a child encounters basic frenzy, it raises her degrees of the anxiety hormones, which are adrenaline and cortisol. Simultaneously, it additionally brings down her "snuggle hormone" oxytocin, which gives a feeling of trust, wellbeing as well as association. Feeling overpowered, she responds by professional challenging—crying, or being requesting. Generally, she is shouting for help. If her parental figure is conflicting in calming her, she stays prepared to dissent—to continue shouting for help until she is able to get it. This inclination describes the individuals who are restlessly connected.

In its outrageous form, these children develop into grown-ups who are inclined to freeze at any trace of good ways from their partner, and perhaps even others, for instance, loved ones.

They become edgy to feel near the other party again and attempt to recapture their partner's attention by escalating their pain (defined as hyperactivating technique). However, even with a steady partner, their fear of rejection can meddle with their inclination console.

If you can even fairly identify with this, you may likewise, at certain times think that it's difficult to unravel your feelings. Rather, you see them as a single upsetting encounter that you can't start to convey or address. With an end goal to adapt to this, you may swear by maladaptive practices, for example, gorging, smoking, drinking, or even drug use.

When attachment related anxiety is an issue, individuals experience various different issues within their attachments that you might identify with. For example, your fear of rejection may keep you from legitimately tending to any contentions or contrasts of assessment with your partner. It may likewise be expending to such an extent that you are not able to imagine the world (or your relationship) through your partner's eyes. Subsequently, you may experience difficulty feeling empathic and steady of your partner (or others).

Moreover, you may experience difficulty really loosening up enough to completely enjoy different parts of your relationship, for instance, your sexual wants—and simply having a ton of fun.

When attachments don't work out, individuals with attachment related anxiety might encounter a requirement for an attachment figure that is exceptional to the point that it, for all intents and purposes, leaks out of their pores. They might dissent furiously, accuse themselves, feel a more noteworthy fascination in their previous partner, and even become distracted with that partner, instead of realizing that a relationship with that individual is dangerous for them. Additionally, they can battle with feeling that they've lost a piece of themselves.

Luckily, if you are sometimes overpowered with attachment related anxiety, you can change this. Additionally, you can alleviate your misery by picking an increasingly secure partner; somebody who can comfort you. Examination proposes that a steady friend might enable a tensely connected individual to feel less anxiety and discouraged, and thus feel more noteworthy fulfillment in her relationship.

Exercise: Can You Relate to "Anxiety and Overwhelmed"?

Think about how much and in what ways you identify with the use of the hyperactivating procedures portrayed in this section. Know that this could take you months of investigation (or even years). However, for the present, I'm just recommending that you investigate the accompanying inquiries so much—or as meager—as you'd like to increase some understanding of how your attachment style influences your feelings. In case you don't have a partner presently, think about it corresponding to a past partner. You may likewise think that it's supportive to distinguish and feature an example by contemplate how these inquiries apply to the whole of your past close attachments.

1. Do you constantly feel that your partner is sincerely far off, or stress that the person in question will leave you? Does this idea

cause you to feel squashed and urgent to keep your partner close (base frenzy)?

2. Even though you probably won't do it intentionally, are you able you perceive how you challenge being disregarded? What are instances of this?

3. Fights regularly reverse discharge, making individuals feel increasingly annoyed or over-whelmed. For every model you gave, clarify how it affected you and potentially even prompted more trouble.

4. Do you battle with feeling vulnerable, awkward, or even imperfect? Think about how your attachment style and fights are identified with this.

5. For certain individuals, being excessively emotional prompts maladaptive methods of adapting, for instance, smoking, drinking, using drugs, or indulging. Do you have maladaptive methods of adapting? If so, how have they been an issue for you?

6. How does your frenzy about being disregarded (if you do freeze) impact your relationship in unfortunate ways, for instance, by making clashes around trust and—deliberately or

subliminally—making it hard for you to unwind and enjoy your partner's conversation?

Feelings? What Emotions?

Kids with a more avoidant style of attachment hinder their emotional responses to dangers, including their base frenzy about the inaccessibility of guardians.

With time, they figure out how to keep their attachment framework deactivated, and they no longer attempt to associate with their folks or battle with partition. Later on during in their lives, they are likewise detached from their partners.

It's imperative to understand that the inclination to divide oneself from feelings doesn't forestall feelings or physiological excitement. It only darkens them. Despite everything, stress hormones flood while oxytocin ("snuggle hormone") levels stay low. Along these lines, even though disregarding, sup-squeezing, or denying feelings might frequently assist with dealing with minor stressors, this methodology is genuinely imperfect.

Whenever individuals with avoidant attachment styles can no longer disregard their feelings because their anxiety or relationship issues have gotten so extreme and determined, they frequently don't have the foggiest idea on how to deal with their feelings. This causes to place them in danger of using undesirable ways to adapt. Their feelings are likewise prone to spill out in spite of their evidently quiet attitude.

For instance, an avoidant man may smoothly discuss his better half being "such a bitch," at the same time denying any resentment, ignorant that his chest is tight and his pulse is up. You should really mull over whether this basic dynamic is what's happening when you think you are quiet however are strangely expressing or doing frightful things. (If your partner will in general be the avoidant one, this dynamic may likewise clarify why you are angry during times when your partner is by all accounts serenely discussing complicated issues.)

The Chemistry of "Secure and Happy"

A few kids are lucky enough to have guardians who reliably support and quiet them whenever they get irritated. The more this occurs, the better they figure out how to go to their folks—and the more they produce the hormone oxytocin, which gives them a feeling of trust, wellbeing as well as association. When kids (and grown-ups) are vexed, oxytocin additionally cuts down their degrees of stress hormones, adrenaline and cortisol too. After some time, these reactions can help them to get settled with the full scope of their feelings and coordinate them into their lives.

They develop struggles safely connected grown-ups who are equipped to deal with their own feelings, tending to individual issues, and viably managing clashes.

It very well may be delighting to find that, as a tensely joined individual, you can "procure" secure attachment—alongside the whole of its benefits. This is something I will address a little bit later in this section. You can likewise reduce your attachment related anxiety and different misery by picking a safely appended partner.

Exercise: Understanding Yourself in Context

The better you see how your hyperactivating or deactivating methodologies created, the more gratefulness you will have on why you do what you do now. As you complete this exercise, show restraint toward yourself. Extending self-understanding can be sustained here, yet it can't be compelled to happen at the same time. So you may need to return to this more than once after some time.

Make note of when you use hyperactivating or deactivating techniques. Come back to your reactions for the past exercise, "Are you able to relate to "Restless and Overwhelmed"?"

Think about them—make sure you possibly talk with somebody you trust. Ensure you have a good handle of your use of hyperactivating methodologies.

If you normally use deactivating systems to keep a separation, you could experience difficulty being explicit about how you do this since you are likely withdrawn from your feelings. Well, I highly recommend that you search for input from individuals you trust and who realize you well.

Try to think about whether you used these equivalent, or comparable, methodologies as a kid. If you did, then think about what may have provoked you to do this. Every now and then you can pick up knowledge about this by thinking about another kid in that equivalent situation.

Model: Jane's last two beaus advised her, "You are simply excessively poor." Although she whined that neither of them was warm, she likewise realized they were right. She was continually apprehensive that they were going to cut off the association, so she would unremittingly call and text them, searching for consolation that they despite everything minded. Whenever she thought about this dynamic, she understood that it helped her to remember how she felt when she was eight years of age and her dad kicked the bucket. From that point onward, she had consistently been apprehensive about drawing near to individuals, since she feared they would leave her.

Once more, don't anticipate that a more deep awareness should show up for the time being. Diary, make notes, and talk with confided individuals about this exercise. Yet in addition give it some rest; then come back to it again after you feel you've gotten an opportunity to develop by and have maybe gotten open to new experiences and viewpoints. With time, a more prominent understanding of your examples can assist you with managing your emotions in an unexpected way, both inside yourself as well as in your attachments.

Two Ways to Earn Security and Happy Relationships

In order to sustain a more beneficial method of connecting in romantic attachments, think about how your current or future relationship may be better if you had a more secure style of attachment. As you think about this, notwithstanding, it's significant for you to realize that you shouldn't be the model of secure attachment to find joy.

Yet, whatever style works for you, it will likely should be a more protected one on the attachment related anxiety and attachment related evasion measurements. Luckily, as I've referenced, you can build up this increasingly secure style as a grown-up. This procedure is the thing that clinicians call "earned security."

There are two fundamental pathways, and they entwine. In the first place, you should look at the outside world. You have to start by building up a relationship with at least one genuinely accessible attachment figure. If not a partner, then you can begin with another person, for example, a relative, friend, minister, or specialist. It could even be God. Make sure you keep in mind, attachment figures are those you believe you can go to in the midst of trouble and who are steady of your efforts to grow your own points of view.

The more you experience feeling acknowledged and ensured, the more you will accept that you are deserving of love as well as that competent others can be accessible to genuinely love and solace you—giving you some "earned security."

The second way to deal with creating "earned security" is to legitimately support a piece of yourself that makes you more mindful of your encounters and to react to those encounters in a more tolerating and caring way.

The way to healthier relationships incorporates a more positive relationship both with yourself and with others. Showing you how to accomplish this, is the thing that the rest of this book is about. To begin with, I'll help you to see more plainly how you propagate your present attachment style in regular day to day existence—and what's kept you from picking a healthier way.

Chapter Three: Open Yourself to Change

Every morning, you look in the mirror with the feeling that you know precisely who is looking back at you. As opposed to have to constantly remind yourself, you simply know what your identity is. This is your personality, and you depend on it to help you to go through every day, similarly as you depend on the ground underneath your feet. When you're not sure about significant parts of your personality you start self-questioning.

Likewise, the more you relate to some parts of your character, the more sure you are to decipher your exercises from that point of view and, afterward, keep on carrying on appropriately. Accordingly, your self-uncertainty, or feeling of insufficiency, can drive you to have struggles and self-censuring. Even though your self-observations and exercises leave you feeling awkward toward yourself, you proceed with the cycle because, at least, it allows you to have a sense of security in having the option to get what you think you need from yourself and others.

It is similarly significant that you have a feeling of consistency about the others characters. Imagine what it resembles to have no clue about whether every individual you meet is what might be compared to Mother Teresa or Jack the Ripper. Those individuals will generally hold opinions about others, right or wrong, in light of specific qualities - man or lady, Caucasian or Hispanic, clerical or hands on specialist. On a much increasingly level, we, as a whole, have opinions about human instinct. For instance, some accept that people will in general be philanthropic while others accept that the vast majority they meet are narcissistic. Such opinions influence the way we approach all relationships - from easygoing to mean ones.

For example, you would likely welcome another friend to your home sooner if you are somebody who accepts that individuals are fundamentally acceptable as opposed to somebody who will in general doubt individuals' honesty or reliability.

The need to see yourself, as well as other people, with a specific goal in mind is significantly comparable to your affection style, since this is a major manner by which you connect with the world. Your mind "triggers" you by giving an image, in light of your specific style, of what you hope to find in your partner, and yourself. Furthermore, it just takes a modest quantity of proof to persuade yourself that your attachment related preferences are detailed, regardless of whether they are genuinely exact or versatile.

For instance, think about Jenny, who has an engrossed style of attachment. She feels insufficient, so she expects that her boyfriends will become worn out on her and afterward he will cheat. Indeed, even with her current sweetheart, Brian, who every now and then communicates his love and frequently attempts to comfort her of his importance, she can't surrender her ground-breaking need to shield herself from any conceivable relinquishment.

So when he got late for a date, she quickly deciphered this as a sign that he was presumably concealing something – most probably a relationship with another woman. To her, this was an additional proof that she was defective and unlovable.

Analysts use the term affirmation predisposition to portray the inclination of individuals to find ways to affirm their own beliefs. When individuals use this inclination to affirm what they accept about themselves (fortunate or unfortunate), analysts call it self-check confirmation. These procedures work for the most part outside of awareness, so individuals can't perceive how their convictions cause them trouble. It's these inconspicuous one-sided observations that cause individuals to repeat old mistakes in the end, even if they lead to agony and failure.

However, individuals now and then become so discontent with their lives or relationships that they start to examine their inclinations - opening up opportunities for change. For example, Jenny had cried over numerous fruitless relationships, never understanding what turned out badly.

However, she detected that Brian truly was an "attendant," so she did some rational soul-looking: she admitted to herself that her feelings of fear of Brian leaving her didn't promise well, given his reliable mindful and steadfastness, and she started then to address and challenge those apprehensions. Even though it didn't fall into place easily requiring some conscious effort on her part, this encouraged Jenny to be increasingly more open to trust Brian and, in the long run, to feel she was adorable. For individuals who experience attachment related anxiety, opening up to the possibility that they are deserving love is particularly significant.

Changing your habit to self-check and view your existence with an affirmation predisposition is difficult, without a doubt. However, you can begin the procedure by realizing what to search for in yourself.

Figuring out how to See Yourself in a Positive Light

It's normal to imagine that you can change your style of relating by simply being careful when you self-check or work from an affirmation inclination, for example, by taking note of when you are superfluously self-basic or feeling when you ridiculously fear rejection. While there is some fact to support this, it's essential to understand that such perceptions can be agitating, or awful; you can feel anxious, instead of thinking about your perceptions; or you simply have a feeling that something is not right.

You are prone to scrutinize these new, more positive perceptions instead of scrutinize your built up inclinations. This is because they offer a point of view that challenges the origin of how you understand yourself and your relationship. Thus, they additionally resent your feeling of comfort and security on the planet.

However, the more you can perceive your inclinations, the more you'll start struggle towards, and even inquiry out, an increasingly target point of view. Gradually you will start to see yourself and your partner in a totally unexpected way.

Affirming the "You" You Know

As said before, individuals are particularly persuaded to confirm their self-view of being worthy or not of love. They do so through specific thought, specific memory, specific understanding. Note how these three standards cover, and all lead to, a similar outcome:

Specific thought: People give more thought to, and invest more energy thinking about, input that affirms their feeling of their own lovability or unlovability than criticism that disconfirms it.

Specific memory: People will in general recall input that affirms their feeling of being worthy or not of love. Sometime they don't process information that don't match with their predisposition.

Specific understanding: People will in general unquestioningly accept criticism that affirms their feeling of being wothy or unworthy. They think that any input that doesn't match with their assumption is wrong or tricky. They likewise decipher missing or questionable proof as help for their self-observations.

As an individual who struggle with attachment related anxiety, you may see that you specifically believe that you are not deserving love in a convoying way: you especially go to find any proof that you are broke, weak, or imperfect; and you make light of, or neglect to see, your qualities or positive properties. Then you recollect things your partner has said or done that appear to confirm that you are inadequate or imperfect in some way, or that he is probably going to reject or leave you. Afterward, you avoid to recall the times your partner revealed to you how brilliant you are or stayed next to you through a hard time.

It may be very hard to find enough point of view to see these inclinations and their impacts on your day by day relationships. So, if you have to, invest some energy investigating and applying this area, alongside the following exercise, to your life.

Exercise: Observe How You Self-Verify

Review the evaluation of your degree of attachment related anxiety in the paragraph "The Basics of How You Connect" in chapter 1. This will show your feeling of your love value.

Answer the accompanying inquiries to better assist you with seeing how you keep up your self-impression of being shameful of love (to the degree that you do feel along these lines). It's a significant step toward breaking the cycle. Complete it corresponding to your partner, just as to other close individuals throughout your life. Repeat the exercise every day until you have a characteristic familiarity with these issues that you experience in your days. Since the effort to self-confirm can make this hard to do, work out your answers as an approach to stay focus and honest to yourself. You may likewise think that it's accommodating to discuss this with your partner or someone else you trust.

Challenging Selective Attention

• What happened during the day you realized that you are worthy of love, or that at least brings into question your self-impression of being unlovable? Pick a couple of situations (for example, your partner needed to sit in front of the TV together, or a friend called you).

• How did you feel in these situations? (For example, glad, awkward, befuddled, nothing.)

• What did you think about these situations? Did you question the trustworthiness of the individual?

(For instance, did you expect your partner needed to stare at the TV with you just without really thinking?)

• Can you perceive how you are and what you feel, checking with particular thought?

Challenging Selective Memory

• What great or positive things did you do today? (Everything checks; nothing is excessively immaterial.)

• In what ways have family, friends, or even associates indicated that they value you?

• In what ways did your partner show that he thinks about you?

Challenging Selective Interpretation

• If you think somebody has generally expressed that you are unlovable, might you be able to misconstrue the other individual's inspiration or goals? (For instance, did you misperceive his sluggishness as your being uninteresting or unlovable?)

• Could you aggravate the input more than expected? (For example, believing you're defective and unlovable when your partner was simply attempting to discuss something that furious him.)

• Are you making light of your qualities and concentrating on ways that you don't satisfy your own unreasonable desires or to the success of your partner and others?

Think about your reactions in every one of the areas above on challenging particular thought, memory, and understanding. Note how you self-confirmed in every one of these ways. What topics do you see? For example, you may turn out envious struggles effectively; or continually get struggles dismissed; or habitually call attention to yourself that you are insufficient, imperfect, or not on a par with your partner. You may likewise battle with the assumption that your partner will stop loving you once he sees the "genuine" you. Or then again you may feel nervous with your partner seeming to not think so much about you. Record in detail the theme(s) that you play out, and clutch this to use them in the exercise "Uncovering Your Invisible Known" in the following part.

Affirming How You See Others

Similarly as individuals unknowingly use affirmation inclination to self-confirm how commendable or dishonorable they believe, they also use it to keep up their feeling of how genuinely accessible or inaccessible their partners (just as others) are.

Basically, individuals who are preconditioned to believe that others won't be there for them will think about themselves as depressed, they think about themselves to be basically alone, and they secure themselves by acting naturally dependent. And subtle and apparently incomprehensible, is the fact that you can also encounter yourself as alone when you accept that others are by and large genuinely benefit capable. This is probably going to happen when you have questions about whether you are deserving to be loved or not, leaving you to feel that those accessible others finally will dismiss you. So even though you may think emphatically about your partner toward the start of your relationship, these discernments will most likely turn negative over the long run, as you find ways to affirm that he truly isn't there for you.

In view of your prejudices about your partner's inaccessibility to you, you are probably going to imagine that a tricky behavior on your partner's part is because of a character strength that won't change, instead of the impact of a situation. For example, if your partner doesn't call one day, you may bounce to the conslusion that it's because of an absence of attention, or even that he is playing with your feelings, rather than the most probable option that he was occupied at work. The more anxiuos you are, the almost certain this will happen when you are feeling awful. This will happen less when you are feeling better or you are essentially cheerful in your relationship.

The inclination toward thinking about others to be depressed makes "vulnerable sides." You just don't "see" how you keep up your conviction that your partner is inaccessible. Similarly as with self-check, your inclination does this through specific thought, specific memory, and specific understanding; however, this time, it's more about the other individual.

Closed Loop Relationships

Each time Dick sees Jane around the house, he criticizes her. Each time Jane sees Dick, she attempts to evade him.

Dick stirs his feelings of prevalence by disapproving Jane. Jane's avoidance strengthens Dick's feelings of predominance.

Jane feeds her feelings of mediocrity by staying away from Dick. Dick's disapproval fortifies Jane's feelings of inadequacy.

Partners keep up a harmony between them that the two of them don't want to change, at least when the relationship is stressed. Every individual reinforce their own self-see by steadily acting in a specific way. This behavior additionally inspires reactions from the other partner that affirm this self-discernment. With such criticism "demonstrating" what they definitely "know" about themselves, individuals again act in accordance with their self-discernments... it's a closed loop.

In a weird manner, the above example of attachment gives both Dick and Jane a feeling of security—they understand what's in store from themselves and one another, and how to react according to that.

This consistency gives comfort even to Jane: how much harder would it be for her if Dick was now and then extremely inclusive? Furthermore, imagine how confusing and awkward it would be for Jane if Dick consistently rewarded her when she deeply accepted that she was unlovable and thought that he would leave her at any second. When others treat you in a way that fits with your self-discernments, you feel approved and the relationship goes on naturally, regardless of whether it is painful. You are likewise bound to proceed with the relationship even if the individual didn't appear to truly "get" you. For instance, as you may know, self-confident individuals who like themselves need to associate with other people who respect them. In any case, and this is may be not as natural, anxious individuals with low confidence frequently leave even when their partners continue seeing them as valuable and adorable. Rather, they will in general stay with and marry less self-confident partners—

which, obviously, just fortifies their feeling of being unlovable. This spots them in a situation where there is lawful and social strain to stay in a relationship that is undesirable for them.

Since such consistency is encouraging, any adjustments in a relationship, even positive ones, are regularly met with opposition. Individuals feel pulled just as by their partners to come back to increasingly unsurprising ways. Even though this attraction to old patterns is solid, individuals can grow new ones. When an individual changes, some former attachments suit to the change, others cease to exist, and new attachments start creating from the "upgraded self." Recognizing and tolerating this fast can facilitate the progress.

A genuine case of this was given in the film Pretty Woman (1990). I'm not discussing the title character, yet about Edward (Richard Gere), a solid, proficient, and very effective agent whose way to deal with life is briskly computing. When he meets a young lady called Vivian (Julia Roberts), she provokes him to open up. He opposes in the beginning, liking to hold his increasingly far off persona. However, with time and the new sincerely close attachment, he turns into a hotter individual. Then he starts to move toward his work more consciously. These progressions unleash devastation. His legal counselor rails against this change, and different "suits" who work for him shy away.

In any case, in excellent Hollywood style, the crowd is left to accept that Edward is a changed man. He weds the lady who has transformed him, and his co-workers must figure out how to conform to the new him, or go antoher way.

Interest Withdrawal: A Common Relationship Problem

One of the most widely recognized risky relationship styles is the interest withdrawal pattern, which develops between a restlessly connected partner (all the more regularly a lady) and an avoidant one. There's a good possibility that you've confronted this situation sooner or later. It works this way: Each time the anxiety partner ventures forward, or inclines in, for closeness, the avoidant partner pulls back, which prompts the anxiety partner to attempt to draw near once more. To get a feeling of how this plays out, think about Lucy and Ken. After dating for about a year, they moved in together.

Tragically, in just a couple of months, their relationship had gotten more stressed:

Lucy: When you get back home, you hardly say hello to me.

Ken: Well, I'm worn out and need an opportunity to simply relax. However, after asking you about your day, you treat me with complete disdain.

Lucy: Sure, you're just worried of having a shower, change clothes, and loosen up some time. In the meantime, I'm taking care of cooking and prepare the table for us, and you never, at any point, offer to help. I got back home from work not that much before you, so I'm worn out, as well.

Ken: (feebly) I've tried to help, yet you don't evene notice that I put everything out on the table.

Lucy: You call that preparing the table? Dropping a napkin and fork close to our seats?! I also need to overlap the napkin and put the fork on it. You always do thing like that, midway, and afterward I need to wrap it up.

Ken: (shrugs his shoulders) No issue what I do, you're just unsettled.

Lucy: I simply wish you just could spontaneously do a few things around the house; and finish what you start.

How hard is that? However, you don't, and I wind up doing everything without anyone else, like the clothing and tidying up and at least, arranging our excursions. You say you love me, however, I don't feel it any longer. I simply feel so alone in everything.

Ken: (as a matter-of-fact way) Well, I guarantee to make a superior effort preparing the table; and I'll accomplish more housework, as well.

Doesn't sound healthy promising, isn't that right? Curiously, the two of them believe they're dealing with the relationship, yet...

Like Lucy, you may get trapped in this example, concentrating on either needing to feel associated or on feeling an absence of association; sometimes times both. Thus you challenge your partner's separation. Lucy does this by requesting and expecting aswers. In any case, her distance from her partner fortifies her feeling of not being loved and her fear that she isn't deserving of love. She does everything she can to battle for her relationship, including making numerous concessions to her partner, yet in addition setting wild eyed expectations for more responsiveness from him.

Their relationships cause her to feel lonely and strengthen her negative thinking about him, and their relationship. Saturated with her own feelings, she doesn't perceive his trouble in light of her requests.

Or then again perhaps you're similar to Ken. You may be for the most part an avoidant individual, however feel anxious as well. An avoidant individual trapped in this example focuses on needing to keep a genuinely protected separation and to evade his partner's indignation or dissatisfaction. Ken is more comfortable and capable when he is autonomous and in a powerful position with Lucy. When she gets furious, he attempts to sincerely remove himself from her and from his own feelings of fear of detachment. He does this by pondering her in a negative manner. He additionally pulls back, turning more firmly to his tendency to act naturally dependent. In doing this, he neglects to perceive or understand Lucy's offers for closeness, warmth, and consolation; or how his absence of emotional expressiveness and absence of warmth cause her to feel horrendously alone.

The most regular long term pattern for these couples is that the two partners become increasingly offensive in their positions. In any case, most of the people, there is, in the end, a flip in their role. Over years, the avoidant individual turns out to be increasingly inaccessible and antagonistic; and the restless individual turns out to be more disturbed like, for example, being unfriendly or taking the decision to leave. In any case, in the middle of stormy occasions, the anxious individual thinks about positive memories and emotions, leading her to connect in a more positive, reconciliatory way. The avoidant partner, however, stays pulled back and furious; he stops any pretense of endeavoring. Regularly, in those couples that got merried, the spouse, who is likely the restless partner, chooses to leave after the kids are grown up and move out (however she doesn't generally hold up that long). Surprisingly, the husband, then, once in a while, frantically seeks after her. Although complex, this is an tremendously normal situation.

The interest withdrawal dynamic turns out badly in certain relationships, which end up being controlling and now and then oppressive. An anxious partner may fall back on getting hostility thought, consolation, or love from an inert and disengaged partner.

At times, it's the avoidant partner who is powerful, however this is all the more frequently indifferent hostility, expressed, for example, in chilly quiet, moving eyes, or different methods of being rude. This behavior is the avoidant partner's method of attempting to get the anxiety partner to ease off.

Exercise: What Would a Fly on the Wall See in Your Home?

Taking note of the emotions, thoughts, and exercises of each partner can assist with giving significant bits of knowledge. Think about the accompanying model:

Jill feels hurt that Paul doesn't invest energy with her on the week-end and rather spends time with his friends. She figures he couldn't care less. She communicates this by crying and telling him he's egotistical. Paul feels assaulted, thinks she is blowing up, and responds by pulling back. Jill feels hurt, and the loop goes on.

In view of this, think about a contention that generally repeat in your relationship. Presently think about the accompanying questions identified with it. (Even though these inquiries expect that you are the one at first annoyed, you can change them to oblige your partner starting the contention.)

As the contention is going on…

FEELING: How are you feeling about what's going on?

THOUGHT: What are you thinking about your partner?

Exercise: How would you express the issue?

FEELING: What do you imagine your partner is feeling on his/her end?

Figured: What do you imagine your partner is thinking about you?

Exercise: How does your partner react?

About the inquiries regarding your partner's understanding, it tends to be useful to ask your partner what he was feeling and thinking, yet, just if you can beneficially discuss this with him. Something else, try identifying with him to imagine his reactions; or approach somebody you trust for help.

Survey Your Patterns

• How would you and your partner influence each other's feelings and exercises?

• What examples do you notice?

• How does this collaboration fortify your convictions about if you deserve to be loved?

• How does this communication strengthen your convictions about how sincerely accessible your partner is?

At a proper, quiet time, you should talk to your partner about this exercise, sharing the bits of knowledge it's given you. You may likewise get some information about how the cooperation's influence his feeling of deserving love and his feeling of how sincerely accessible you are.

This is a territory that you may find accommodating to invest some energy investigating in. You may likewise think that it's accommodating to thoroughly think about this now for some time, then come back to at it again in the near future.

Summary: Gaining Perspective

In this part, I have indicated how your attachment style, self-check, and the affirmation inclination consolidate to keep you repeating old mistakes. They misshape your observations and bolster every now and then counterproductive methods of review yourself and your partners (past, present, and future). That is a way to attempt to understand and truly ingest.

To completely get it, you have to invest some energy turning it over in your psyche. Also, you totally need to apply it to how you've carried on with your life, and keep on doing as such.

In the following section, I spread out a greater amount of the low down about how conceivable it is to know whole the information in a theoretical way and still be oblivious to your tricky methods of connecting on the planet. This understanding can help make you fully aware of the ways you can break the pattern and set up more joyful, more beneficial relationships.

Chapter Four: Dealing With Obstacles

When individuals know about their relationship patterns and are persuaded to change, they frequently unconsciously sabotage their efforts at personal development. For example, Vito loved Miranda and realized that his extraordinary (and unjustified) desire upset her. He is stressed that he would drive her away, so he decided to trust her, particularly after she yelled at him for sneaking around on her smartphone. Many weeks later, however, he indiscreetly got Miranda's telephone to check whether she had been messaging other men. With her just in the following room, this behavior showed up obtrusively worthless, yet that was surely not the purpose. He started with this behaviour, suddenly, after he saw a previous partner joyfully holding the hand of a man at the shopping center. Even though misinformed and unsafe, his brisk look at Miranda's telephone was really his effort to assist himself with recovering his conviction that all is good.

As I've noticed, individuals need to know that all is well with the world to work in day by day life. The drive to find it out is particularly increased when you are frightened of losing your partner.

This can trigger you to experience once more the equivalent basic anger you may have felt as a newborn child, when each peril undermined your endurance and you urgently looked for your folks to comfort and secure you. At the end of the day, when you sense that your partner probably won't be there for you, you can feel frightened to death. Or on the other hand when you try to change in ways that contrast with your attachment style, which is intended to protect you, you are probably going to naturally come back to your previous, well-known, attachment practices—regardless of whether those practices (like Vito's) are counterproductive and go against your conscious promise to "improve." This method of understanding behavior isn't generally instinctive and can be confusing. So let's investigate.

Self-Deception

Individuals' attachment styles and attachment related practices are part of their identity, and can be so firmly inspired by base anger that it is amazingly hard for them to perceive all the way by which they self-check, at least, when they know to search for this predisposition.

For example, some tensely joined individuals start drinking alcohol as an approach to mitigate their pain in the wake of feeling dismissed. In the end, when this behaviour goes too far into alcohol abuse, they frequently don't understand or recognize the full degree of their concern, since that would just irritate them more. Also, numerous restlessly connected ladies accuse themselves when they are shoved and beaten by their partner, something that happens regularly, and therefore they decide to stay in that relationship.

Additionally, incensing to spectators is the hit or miss affirmation of issues. For example, think about Linda. She thought she had "everything", a loving spouse, magnificent children, and no financial concerns, yet, she was discouraged. She was likewise furious with herself since she didn't think she deserved any option to be miserable. However, she felt her partenr didn't respect her, and that she'd dedicated her life to him (and others) so much that she didn't do anything for herself, thus she felt denied. When some of those statements were repeated, she reacted as though she was hearing it just because. "I recently said that, isn't that right? Amazing." But just a couple of moments later, she was again mourning that she didn't have the foggiest idea why she was so troubled.

She obviously knew, in some way or another, that these battles existed, or she was unable to have informed me regarding them.

In any case, she additionally couldn't let them dwell completely and peacefully in her awareness. In this way, it could be said, she realized them, yet didn't have any acquaintance with them. You experience this when you sense that something clashes with your attachment style, yet don't completely recognize it. It's a defensive method of removing you from a mental danger or emotional agony (a dynamic regularly alluded to by specialists as "separation"). You can likewise get a feeling of "knowing-however not-knowing" along these lines: Think about somebody who got thought as a newborn child just when she turned out struggles deeply emotional. In light of this early experience, she may proceed with an example of being excessively emotional with others well into adulthood. Even though she's mindful of being an emotional individual, she doesn't deliberately realize that is her method of drawing near to other people, which stands out from Linda's fractional attention to why she was troubled.

I call both of these knowing however not-knowing encounters, the imperceptible known.

When you battle with understanding why it's so difficult to change how you act in relationship, think about pondering your past as an approach to take advantage of the undetectable known.

Since patterns are built up depending on past encounters (with youth frequently having a solid impact), individuals now and then react to current situations such that possibly bodes well when one thinks about their past. On Linda's account, she spent her youth attempting uselessly to satisfy her mom, who cruelly rewarded her. Because of this, it was not hard to see how she built up a style of being ideal to individuals and striving to evade their anger. While her "excellence" helped her to make numerous friends, it additionally much of the time left her inclination irrelevant. Of course, she battled with the imperceptible known and couldn't talk genuinely to her better half about numerous worries between them, worries that got accumulated throughout the years. In the end, she got upset enough to start looking for a treatment.

Shockingly, when you have unfortunate methods of adapting or identifying with others, your efforts to fix issues and adapt regularly become an endless loop. They exacerbate the situation, and spread the closed circle patterns talked about in the last part. Linda's situation is a open case of this. She reacted to her fear of rejection by being additionally good, yet this prompted her inclination insignificant and dismissed, which she reacted to by investing much more energy. Additionally, the difficult consumer uses alcohol to quiet his pain, which brings more issues and more misery. He reacts by again attempting to numb himself with more alcohol, accordingly beginning the circle once more—even if his marriage self-destructs and his ability to work break down. Also, as any unreasonably perfectionistic individual will let you know, the harder he attempts to get everything right, the more issues he sees with his exhibition.

The Logic Stops Here

You may think: "Alright, I get the whole undetectable known thought, yet, why can't individuals simply change once these encounters are found out?" This appears smart, like having the option to open a safe once you're given the key. However, it is difficult.

The very intricacy that empowers you to build up your personality, with the goal that you can work generally effectively in your life, additionally often makes such straightforward plans incapable. Individuals frequently have clashing thoughts or convictions, or get criticism that conflicts with their beliefs; and such clashes causes' internal pressure that experts call intellectual discord. It's a very awkward encounter that individuals unwittingly put everything on the line to escape. In their book Mistakes Were Made, analysts Carol Tavris and Elliot Aronson clarify: "it could be said, discord hypothesis is a hypothesis of vulnerable sides, of how and why individuals unexpectedly shock themselves with the goal that they neglect to see crucial, and information that may toss them into cacophony, making them question their behavior or their feelings".

To see how this influences your attachment style and relationships, recall that you build up your attachment style to have a sense of security and confidence on the planet.

This starts to frame during our youth and is fortified through day by day encounters over a lifetime of self-check and affirmation predisposition; your try to demonstrate that you are who you think you are (for example, disgraceful of love) and that others are who you think they are (for example, accessible attachment figures). To explain, think about a anxiously connected lady with low confidence. She may quickly like her boyfriend applauding her, yet this will make subjective cacophony. So she will rapidly return to review herself harmfully, complete with a variety of motivations to support why she's "undeserving"; all of this settle her discord without anyone else checking (and fortifying) her negative mental self-portrait. This is the way by which psychological disharmony and self-check cooperate to square change. How individuals feel about past occasions can shield them from relinquishing those occasions and cause them to act in undesirable way or to battle with specific situations. For example, the way that a lady mentally realizes that she was explicitly mishandled as a kid doesn't mysteriously calm her of the emotional torment from those encounters, anything else than realizing that somebody hit you over the head with a block can mend your fractured skull.

So, she may attempt to desist from thinking about those encounters even as she keeps on feeling awkward with physical closeness. In situations like this, when individuals are forced to keep away from emotional agony, or the explanations behind it, they are left to exist with the uknown, which has its own annoying torment, and to indiscriminately repeat dangerous practices or encounters.

While it may appear to work well to encourage yourself to "simply let it go" this advice is pointless,or worst. Nobody needs to feel upset; accepting that you are deliberately tormenting yourself just adds anger to your torment.

Indeed, even individuals who are distinctively avoidant and generally great at denying emotional agony despite everything, need to battle with the unknown when it turns out struggles so excruciating or disastrous that they are forced to confront it. For example, Laura was a housewife who used self-restraint to keep up method for herself and to assist her with imposing method on her family. Nonetheless, as her kids grown up more established, they started to challenge her control and she started to lose her temper.

Their developing freedom released her feelings and her self-questions (which she had seldom even recognized to herself). Her misery made it unusual for her to stay easily confident and discovered exactly how alone she had felt in her marriage. Some place somewhere inside her, she had realized that she felt inaccessible from her better half—and that she was responsible for this separation.

To completely recognize and address the undetectable, individuals should steadily challenge the guidelines that they verifiably live by, for example, expecting that others won't genuinely love them and be there for them. For example, Laura was capable to recognize that she never really completely confided in her better half, so she had generally excused his mindful motions and contemplated how he let her down. As she gambled being helpless by telling this to her better half, she found that he was understanding and furthermore willing for a closer relationship. By opening up to meet yourself as well as other people in an unexpected way, you can start to slacken your solid grasp on the past and recuperate from old damages. This can assist you with changing how you identify yourself, as well as other people does.

Exercise: Revealing Your Invisible Known

The last part helped you to recognize manners by which you self-confirm. Audit your answers or complete the exercise once more.

Presently, for this current part's exercise, we'll make it a step further.

Make note of a subject or two that you decided to concentrate on. Read the topics that you distinguished while finishing that exercise in the last section. Then, reconnect with your perceptions of how you self-confirmed to play them out.

Ask yourself:

• How did you feel as you verified your specific thought, specific memory, and specific translation (for example, pressure, distress)?

- How did your inclination influence your convictions about yourself?

Uncovering your undetectable known, you may find that you can see your inclination, yet lose your attention to it as you get sucked into the predisposition itself.

For instance, you may see that you will in general excuse your partner's actual mindfulness as his simply meeting a promise. But instead than permit yourself to perceive that your predisposition shields you from being available to the chance of his love, you may become involved with demonstrating to yourself that he doesn't generally adore you and that he may leave whenever. Seeing your predisposition and afterward having it vanish is a proof of the unknown. It's much the same as an enchantment stunt, presently you see it, presently you don't!

Practice this exercise over and over with various instances of similar topics. Repeating it will assist you with getting more conscious of how your imperceptible known coordinates your feelings and practices. It will likewise assist you with seeing your part in your relationship issues.

It is exceptionally useful and illuminating to share your perceptions, thoughts, and emotions with somebody trustworthy in your life—possibly your partner. Journaling about them can likewise help.

How Pain Motivates Change

When individuals with a restless attachment style overperform with an end goal to demonstrate their worth, they are frequently try to shroud their fear of rejection and their feeling of imperfection. Each time these issues repeat, they are unwittingly pushed into the famous wardrobe, away from consciousness (as referenced prior, numerous specialists allude to this as separation). Inevitably the "garbage" (and issues identified with it) pushes to come out, like the mainstream drawing of a protruding entryway of an overstuffed wardrobe. Individuals respond to their developing misery in many different way, for example, encountering wretchedness, anxiety, sleep deprivation, general weakness, or interminable back agony. They may likewise indulge, misuse alcohol, or overshopping.

When you can mentally perceive that a specific predisposition causes you trouble, you may not give a lot of genuine thought to it. Rather, you experience a feeling of realizing that it is "only the status quo." You may "know" that you are unlovable, and you may likewise "know" that others won't dependably be there for you.

As Robert Burton (2008) successfully contended in his book 'On Being Certain: Believing You Are Right Even When You're Not' individuals' feeling of knowing is outside their ability to be in control and can't be effortlessly contended away. It's a groundbreaking pull for them to stay as they've generally been, at least, when they are participating in pointless practices.

For example, anxiously joined individuals with low confidence can tune in into exhortation on the most proficient method to develop themselves; they can think positive thoughts; they can put themselves in a huge number of ways to feel better; however, all without any result. On a deep level, they "know" that they are unsatisfactory in some basic way. Keep in mind that they built up their character after some time, and that it supplies them with a feeling of wellbeing. In any case, in the long run, a significant number of them feel so much misery that they are compelled to think that something must change, regardless that they don't have the foggiest idea what it is. Indeed, even avoidant individuals, who generally keep up an in-control way, are now and then pushed out of their customary range of familiarity by serious and constant stress factors.

The feelings of being distant from everyone else and helpless that they have safeguarded against their whole lives, bomb them, thus they are induced to become consious of the emotional agony. At these occasions, they are generally willing—if not actually emotional—to take a stab at something else.

So whatever your attachment style is, you are probably going to stir things up simply in the wake of feeling critical misery or emotional torment. By facing the challenge of truly observing and testing current predispositions of yourself, as well as other people, you allow yourself to think about new viewpoints. One of my patients shared an astute statement to clarify why she finally came to treatment, following a while of battling with this contention: "And the day came when the risk to stay tight in the bud was more painful than the risk that it took to bloom." (The wellspring of this citation is obscure, however it has at times been ascribed to Anaïs Nin.)

The Need for New Experiences

Feeling emotional torment and seeing how you keep up risky patterns, don't reveal to you how to appear different or naturally build up more beneficial examples.

This needs to create new ones start after some time with new encounters. For instance, you may understand that you will in general be watched with everybody in your present life, even your life partner, since you felt condemned or sincerely deserted as a child by your friends; or because a previous partner went behind your back with your dearest friend. However, after you understand this: you, despite everything, have a couple of tasks to accomplish if you need to change. In a mindful relationship, you should allow yourself to let down your protections and experience weakness. Then you'll have to build up the inward strength to keep connecting with you partner, after you feel hurt by him/her (which will inevitably happen in any cozy relationship). Yet, there's no compelling reason to stress a lot about this. Simply continue gradually. You'll need to feel yourself stretch, however, less that you snap.

To delineate further, think about Jessie. Her folks loved her, however they were ordinarily, fairly and genuinely far off. They could laugh and snicker and have an "ordinary" family life, yet they would in general spotlight on their children successes as opposed to on identifying with their characteristics and encounters.

When Jessie and her kin were pitiful or harmed or troubled in any ability, her folks reacted with mandates not to whimper and with a draw yourself-up-by-the-bootstraps attitude.

Jessie learned not to complain. She came to accept that her defective exhibition and upsetting emotions implied that she wouldn't be loved, yet, additionally, that she was basically imperfect and shameful of love. Regardless of what achievements she accomplished throughout everyday life (and there were many), she never felt adequate. She was continually trusting that others will see her mistakes and perceive her shamefulness, rejecting her. Sadly, this likewise implied she didn't confide in any man who demonstrated enthusiasm for her, except if he was additionally dismissing, somehow or another. As you would imagine, the relationships she had with men were brief and painful.

For Jessie, in the same way as other individuals who are grown up in families that make acknowledgment dependent upon execution, acting naturally was a method of adapting that seemed well and good—she was attempting to fix all the issues in her presentation so her relatives would be pleased with her and love her.

As a grown-up, her "overlearned" self-analysis was a piece of her personality that she used to attempt to help herself in two significant ways. First, by barely concentrating on how she could improve her presentation; she could, once in a while, stay away from the horrendous trouble of realizing she was not exactly great and unlovable. Second, she legitimately attempting to avoid rejection, which she thought would occur if she failed in any ability. Also, to wrap things up, her additional efforts sometimes paid off in others' being content with her presentation (not that she could permit herself to completely take this in).

When Jessie started treatment, she was liberated from her self-assaults, yet she was unable to make sense of how to get away. She was mindful that the wish for a more beneficial and joyful method of being, doesn't in itself uncover a guide for how to achieve it. To desert those old, thrashed, and roundabout ways, you should plan a successful departure course (or be helped by somebody who has such a plan). For Jessie, that course was figuring out how to esteem herself, not exactly what she could achieve. When she succeeded in doing this, she had the option to desert her basic self, and allow herslf to build a mind-blowing relationships.

Obviously, as with such a great amount throughout everyday life, "the overlooked details are the main problem." The following section will offer some fundamental rules on how you can build up a customized escape course.

Chapter Five: Lasting Security Path

By this point in the book, you realize your attachment style. You understand what makes you sustain undesirable and inadequate methods of seeing yourself and your partner. These are critical experiences. Nevertheless, as you increase your awareness, you will likewise feel a solid draw to self-check the old view of yourself. You'll find ways to keep seeing yourself, your partner, and your relationship as you generally have, and to oppose the conceivably healing impact of what you are finding out about yourself. In case you continue, however, another point of view will win. You will be more liberated to figure out how to support a more joyful relationship, and possibly change your attachment style. While this offers extraordinary expectation, the billion-dollar question is how to do it—how can you keep up understanding into unfortunate examples and really (finally) support a cheerful relationship?

When confronted with this inquiry, it's normal for individuals to search for explicit replies answers—a list of safeguard systems or strategies to meet these difficulties. They search for solid devices: Do this. Don't do that. Regularly, however, the immediate techniques alone fall flat.

Individuals can't successfully use the "great" counsel they are given since their internal condition bolsters the unfortunate norm.

What's required is an approach to change that center condition—which is a way that straightforwardly improves how you identify with yourself and sincerely associate with your partner. This makes me think about what occurred with a little plant I once had. Its green leaves gave my office a little warmth, notwithstanding its absence of flowers. In any case, when I moved to an office with an enormous mass of windows that confronted the morning sun, pink flowers detonated on top of it and lit up my office, just like my state of mind. Correspondingly, individuals can get the "daylight" they have to bloom from loving relationships.

If you are continually staying in the shadows of your attachment related anxiety, there are two different ways you can find joy in your relationships—and even "gain" secure attachment. One route is with a genuinely accessible attachment figure who is loving, tolerating, as well as reliably accessible. This could be a romantic partner, yet not really.

This figure could likewise be a relative, a friend, a pastor, a specialist, a coach, or even God. To be honest, it very well may be anybody whom you feel that you can go to for help.

The other path is through what I call merciful awareness—which is an attention to yourself from the point of view of having a worry for, and a craving to reduce, your own misery. In both cases, love leaks in after some time to comfort and promise you that you are deserving of it. Finally, in order to acquire secure attachment, you should be available to adore from a genuinely accessible attachment figure and be available to being sympathetically mindful.

Luckily, a genuinely loving partner is able to assist you with creating caring awareness; and humane awareness can assist you with being increasingly open to a really loving partner. Each of these can expand on the other—a tad at once—to assist you with feeling increasingly deserving of affection, see your partner in a more positive light, and work with your partner to sustain a glad and healthy relationship.

And, they can assist you with creating a sense (or, more precisely, a psychological portrayal) of your partner—and finally yourself—that you can convey with you any place you go, which can comfort and console you in the midst of misery. The possibility of having the right partner can assist you with feeling cherished and glad is the thing that fantasies—and romantic stories—are made of. You can naturally get it. Yet, humane awareness needs some clarifying. The idea became out of my biting interest in what different zones of mental writing (not simply the ones that I was aware of) needed to state about making individual change. Sympathetic awareness introduced itself as imperatively significant in close to home change as well as healing. Its two principle components are awareness and self-compassion, the two of which I will clarify inside and out underneath.

Awareness

To improve your close relationships, you should look at your job in making issues—or at what you do to keep relationships from the beginning.

However, as I've clarified, individuals' inclinations will in general visually impaired them to these bits of knowledge. So, creating awareness and using it tends struggles dubious.

Yet, if you continue watching your inclination to affirm your predispositions of both yourself and your partner (or possible partner), you will start to see these inclinations more effectively and more unmistakably. Done mixing up discernments as essential fact of the matter, you will be more liberated to start positive changes.

It's useful to think about awareness as included awareness of feelings, familiarity with thoughts as well as mentalizing—all of which I will depict beneath.

Familiarity with Emotions

Feelings give a lavishness of experience that would be deficient in an absolutely educated presence. It's the distinction, for example, between realizing another romantic intrigue is a solid match for you on paper and really feeling joyous beyond words. By opening up to feelings, individuals can now and then distinguish convictions or encounters that they were already uninformed of, or that they didn't understand the strength of.

For instance, a lady may understand she is infatuated with a friend simply subsequent to feeling aches of envy about his dating another person. Another model is a lady who realizes she loves investing energy alone, yet possibly acknowledges exactly how significant is the point at which her new sweetheart becomes tenacious. Feelings not just revive presence; they additionally give information to us to follow up on.

Alongside being in contact with their feelings, individuals should have the option to self-control—or oversee—them so they don't get too over-whelmed. They attempt to do this in various manners, a significant number of which fall flat—and some of which you may identify with. For instance, they may attempt to stifle, deny, or numb troubling feelings. In any case, when those strategies are used again and again, the emotions are probably going to go under-ground, just to return out sometime in the not too distant future—and furiously, regularly leaving individuals anxiety, discouraged, or irate. An alternate methodology is when individuals ruminate, over and over again surveying the causes and results of an issue as they search for an answer.

However, when the issue has no genuine or clear answer, they stay trapped in a pattern of feeling irritated and anxiety, attempting to issue illuminate in order to lessen their pain, neglecting to fix their concern, and afterward feel more anxiety. Or then again they become so overpowered that the entirety of their feelings feels like one major rock mounted immovably on their chest.

On the other hand, individuals who self-direct viably can endure and acknowledge their feelings. They may use the adapting systems I mentioned above, yet they do it without neutralizing themselves in different manners. For example, they may smother their feelings while at work, yet permit themselves to get resentful about home and discussion about their emotions with both their partners and others. Since they don't feel especially undermined by their pain, they don't safeguard too firmly against it. This permits them struggles more completely mindful. Thus, they can ride the flood of their feelings as opposed to feeling like they are suffocating in them.

In order to help explain, think about somebody who is lamenting over the demise of a dear friend.

If this individual is scared by or needs to avoid his misery, he may stop his feelings, leaving him stuck in emotional deadness (however shielded from the agony) and incapable to genuinely associate with others in a deep manner. Conversely, somebody who is more tolerating of sorrow is commonly ready to impart it to friends and family and keep up sincerely cozy relationships. Albeit battling with antagonistic feelings is consistently difficult, the individuals who can self-manage adequately don't feel emotional anguish (trouble about their pain) as much as individuals who battle their feelings.

Once in a while, people believe that recognizing a difficult situation implies that they then need to either be surrendered to it or follow up on it. If they are not set up to do it is possible that, they attempt to deny their experience. Also, finally, they stay upset without an approach to address it.

For example, Amelia wouldn't like to acknowledge that her significant other is heartless to her since she fears that she would then need to either leave him, which she isn't prepared to do, or forever surrender to being troubled. In fact, her feelings don't mean both of these things.

They just imply that she is troubled at the present time. Whenever she recognizes and acknowledges this, she will feel in a state of harmony with herself, which will give her an alternate point of view on her concern. She will probably grow both new acknowledge and alternatives—like finding she would really be more joyful without him, or that they can chip away at their marriage together. Obviously, she can generally choose to surrender to the situation; yet and, after its all said and done she would do it with an alternate outlook, which may empower her to deliberately choose the most ideal ways to proceed within the marriage.

Recognizing Thoughts and Emotions

It is essential to know the distinction among thoughts and emotions. You might be amazed to find that numerous individuals confuse them. For instance, it would not be extraordinary for somebody to say, "I have a feeling that I was excessively calm on that date." This, obviously, is an idea and definitely not a feeling. Feelings are a mix of being stimulated with a certain goal in mind and the importance we put to that excitement. Therefore, you may feel humiliated about not saying much on a date.

When individuals botch their thoughts for feelings, their genuine feelings stay unexplored. Basically, perceiving this misstep and afterwards concentrating on feelings, regularly drives individuals to encounter themselves in an increasingly emotional manner. For instance, when you understand you feel humiliated, you may likewise acknowledge your fear of being judged. And afterward, you can look for consolation or backing; or you may understand that your fear is superfluous.

In order to represent how poor emotional awareness can be an issue, think about a situation that oftentimes happens in treatment. A lady—let's use the name Maxine—is battling with her better half's unfaithfulness. She says, "I have a feeling that I can't confide in him any longer. Furthermore, truly, in what ability am I able to do this? He would disclose to me he was busy working when he was truly… "And off she goes, revealing to me about the terrible things he has done. Her discourse is quick and she sounds irate—the more she talks, the more furious, overpowered, and confused she becomes. Despite of being emotional, her doubts and the instances of his untruthfulness are thoughts and not emotions. So I pull her together on what she is feeling.

With some provoking, she recognizes feeling furious, double-crossed, dismal, frightened, and hurt. She cries as she connects with these feelings; and she feels heard. In spite of the platitude of an advisor attempting to get patients to cry, my center (and the accommodating piece of this exchange) is to connect her with her emotions and assist her with feeling heard; crying is only the inescapable result of her doing that. Regardless of whether she needs to take a shot at fixing her marriage, she is in contact with the torment that requires recuperating, thus she can start to chip away at facilitating that torment.

Exercise: Opening Up to Emotion

Entwined with naming your feelings is the way that you recognize them. You should step out of your encounters enough to have the option to understand them. This venturing out diminishes your submersion in your feelings—regardless of whether it is just for a second. To enable you to understand, think about how you feel at this moment. Truly, kindly do that at the present time. I can hold up a moment. Notice how you moved from contemplation of concentrating on your feelings focusing on your emotions and thinking about the name for them.

This ability to move thought can be useful in allowing you to have your feelings while not getting devoured by them—particularly when they're solid emotions.

This is the most ideal approach to practice with low-power feelings, which have to a lesser degree a possibility of overpowering you. Similarly as you halted minutes back to think about your feelings, make it a training to do this at several occasions during your day. For instance, you can do it at supper time, before going out in the first part of the day, or after showing up at your office. The significant point is for you to figure out how to direct the experience your feelings—uplifting your attention to them, and moving between being in them and intentionally watching them.

With training, you will be better ready to do this with increasingly exceptional feelings. Also, the better you are at doing it, the more liberated you will be to see your situation with some viewpoint—and maybe think about elective ways to either understand or react to your situation.

If, in the same way as other individuals, you experience some difficulty distinguishing your particular feelings, don't stress out. That is a typical issue, and one that an exercise in the following part will address.

Attention to Thoughts

How you experience yourself and your convictions about yourself is highly influenced by your reasoning. For example, you fortify self-questions and low confidence when you repeat convictions, for example, "Danny doesn't generally cherish me. He just stays with me since he feels frustrated about me." Those thoughts additionally trigger feelings, for instance, trouble and fear of rejection.

Regardless of whether you understand it or not, you have a constant running subtext of thoughts. Bringing that subtext to cognizance can be incredibly useful in figuring out how you sustain misery inside yourself and your relationship. With that awareness, you additionally have a chance to take a shot at change. Once in a while, even only the awareness itself, is sufficient to encourage change.

Exercise: Experimenting with Your Thoughts

This straightforward exercise is an incredible exhibition of how your reasoning influences you on numerous levels. Locate a calm spot to finish it. It will take just a couple of moments.

Sit easily, take a full breath or two, and make sure you close your eyes.

Gradually examine your body from your toes up to the highest point of your head. Know about any sensations, for example, muscle pressure, the vibe of breathing, or your heart thumping.

Infer a negative idea about yourself. Pick one that you will in general battle with. Hold it in your brain and then repeat it.

Focus on how this influences you. What sensations do you feel? How can it influence your feelings and your thoughts?

Well, you will feel more terrible when you focus on negative self-observations. You may see expanded snugness in your chest or agitating in your stomach. You may likewise know about inclination dismal or irate with yourself, or having a course of other negative thoughts. Presently do this exercise once more—but somewhat better. Prior to starting, think about when you liked yourself. What positive thoughts did you have about yourself? Use these thoughts as the concentration as you complete this exercise. Generally, if you will act naturally basic or delayed to value your positive characteristics, you will locate this harder to do.

However, in doing it, you will see more positive encounters (regardless of whether they're short lived, for example, increasingly loosened up muscles, a feeling of being lighter or more joyful, and possibly more positive thoughts).

Mentalizing

The third, and last, some portion of awareness is mentalizing, which is a procedure related with psychoanalyst Peter Fonagy together with his partners. They have clarified this as a procedure wherein individuals experience themselves and the world through their psyches. This allows them to take an intelligent position—to think about the mental explanations behind their own and others' behavior. Critically, however, mentalizing likewise includes being genuinely associated while having that smart position. The individuals who have a solid mentalizing ability sense that they can change the idea of their encounters by contemplating them in an unexpected way.

The supposition that individuals have shared encounters is verifiable in mentalizing.

This normal mankind, as depicted by specialist Kristin Neff (2008), normally gives individuals a feeling of association and understanding for themselves as well as other people. They can feel sympathy and empathy for those in torment since they can relate.

Over and over again, in any case, restlessly connected individuals don't completely feel that they are a piece of this basic mankind. Therefore, while they may understand why others do and feel as they do (it's just being human), they don't have any significant bearing this equivalent understanding to themselves. And, even if they have sympathy for other people, they experience themselves as imperfect such that causes them to feel undeserving of empathy—and over and over again slanted to blame themselves for relationship issues. However, after some time, their repeated understanding of feeling dismissed—at least, when their partners are not significant to dismiss them—drives them to react by being reproachful of their partners. To help explain how mentalizing can be influenced by attachment related anxiety, think about the way Sydney—a lady with a solid engrossed style—responds after an arranged meet up disregards her conspicuous readiness to meet once more.

Naturally, she is despondent about this. Nevertheless, in light of her powerless ability to mentalize, she compares the feeling of rejection with her being imperfect and disgraceful of adoration. She feels despaired and isolates herself. However, if her attachment related anxiety were less exceptional, her ability to understand the situation with more point of view won't probably be so hindered. She could feel hurt while perceiving that not every person clicks—and that being dismissed doesn't make her a reject. She may even recall that there are men she's enjoyed or regarded in the past who didn't intrigue her impractically.

While reinforcing her ability to mentalize can assist Sydney with opening up positive perspectives about herself and her relationships, it shockingly doesn't consequently ease trouble. Quite frequently, individuals feel that they should never again be vexed once they understand their situation. In my clinical practice, it isn't strange for patients to state something like, "I know I'm generally terrified of being judged because my dad was brutal when I was a kid. In any case, that was happening a while back and he's dead at this point. So why wouldn't i be able to simply get over it as of now?" The appropriate response is that a few things in life are difficult, and no measure of understanding will change that. In any case, figuring out how to react with self-compassion might alleviate that hurt and assist you with pushing ahead throughout everyday life.

Mentalizing can sound convoluted; and it generally is. In any case, you as of now practice it in your life while thinking abouting your feelings as you think about why you do what you do, or why others do what they do. In the following part, I will offer exercises to explicitly build up your mentalizing ability.

Self-Compassion

Awareness—which incorporates awareness of feelings, familiarity with thoughts as well as mentalizing—is a useful asset, yet it can't help you without anyone else. So, we should investigate the other portion of the recipe for making successful, enduring change—self-compassion.

Individuals don't simply get themselves or have feelings or think thoughts; they just identify with these encounters. When individuals acknowledge themselves and become friends with their feelings, it is quite normal for them to treat themselves with generosity and identify themselves with self-compassion.

Even though individuals don't speak much about self-compassion, they frequently talk about empathy, which is something you feel for another person who is irritated.

It includes imagining another person's perspective, or having sympathy, and needing to ease their anguish. Self-compassion is just taking that equivalent position with yourself.

Specialist Kristin Neff (2008) is at the front line of investigating self-empathy and its suggestions as well. She characterizes it as having three fundamental parts: self-thoughtfulness, basic humankind, and mindfulness.

Self-Kindness

This is exactly what it seems like—being caring to yourself. Individuals who grasp this strength are delicate with themselves when they experience torment, disappointment, or deficiency. Instead of losing control or being incredulous of themselves in these conditions, they react with understanding and delicacy. They want to treat themselves well, to satisfy quick delight, yet struggles sound, cheerful individuals as long as possible. Therefore, while they are benevolent and tolerating of themselves at the time, they are additionally inspired to improve.

These last focuses are critical. Numerous individuals fear that self-benevolence may prompt being lethargic or smug, or either letting themselves free without any issue. However, genuine self-compassion—like empathy as a rule—isn't just a quest for sure fire satisfaction. Think about some notable merciful individuals whom you likely think about with deference: Buddha, Gandhi, Jesus, Martin Luther King Jr., Mother Teresa, Nelson Mandela. Their incredible sympathy roused them to work perseveringly in helping other people experience a more prominent feeling of wellbeing—and accomplishing driven objectives could be a piece of that. Similarly, self-compassion will normally rouse you to seek after inward development.

It's additionally critical to understand that acting in a natural way doesn't mean being childish. When you are self-kind, you mind especially about others just as about your own needs. In any case, this occasionally implies concentrating on your own issues first. Christopher Germer (2009, 89) communicates this well in his book The Mindful Path to Self-Compassion: "In a room brimming with individuals, it bodes well to help the individual who's enduring the most, the one we know best, the one we're generally fit to make a difference. Some of the time that individual is you… "

Basic Humanity

This is the acknowledgment that all individuals share basic encounters, for example, torment and enduring, shortcomings and flaws. By feeling associated with others along these lines, individuals feel less detached and less forlorn. They understand that their issues are just part of being human, and that these troubles don't imply that there is something basically amiss with them. So instead of being buried in self-centeredness, those with a solid feeling of regular mankind will in general feel all the more alright (however not really cheerful) about their battles.

Mindfulness

This is a nonjudgmental awareness of thoughts and emotions without attachment to them. Not all the conversation of awareness of thoughts and emotions are in the "Mindfulness" area above, mindfulness concentrates more on the procedure of mindfulness—how you approach and treat your encounters—than on investigating and separating the encounters themselves. When you are careful, you are genuinely at the time. You acknowledge encounters without the need to deny, stifle, or even misrepresent them.

You additionally have viewpoint on your encounters, more self-empathy, and a more noteworthy feeling of wellbeing during unpleasant occasions.

The advantages of mindfulness become particularly obvious when you think about what happens when individuals are not careful. For instance, individuals who are effortlessly activated to feel overpowered with a feeling of rejection regularly lose point of view and excessively relate to their thoughts and emotions. They respond by being tenacious or lashing out of frustration. In both cases, they drive their partners further away—something contrary to the closeness that they really want. Also, if they attempt to stifle their negative feelings, those emotions frequently return with much more noteworthy force. On the other hand, if these individuals figured out how struggles increasingly careful, they would feel less overpowered, even in the midst of upsetting feelings, and could get themselves and their responses better. Consequently, they could react in more beneficial, increasingly helpful ways, for example, by conversing with their partners about their battles and legitimately requesting consolation (Wallin, 2007).

As Neff (2008) accentuates, self-compassion can't happen without self-benevolence, normal humankind, as well as mindfulness. Individuals must experience self-generosity; they should be persuaded to follow up for their own sake toward a feeling of wellbeing. They should understand and feel that they are a piece of a typical mankind wherein each individual battles similarly as they do. Additionally, finally, they should be careful so they can know about their encounters without being overpowered by them. These three components together can assist you with nurturing a positive feeling of yourself, a more prominent suspicion that is all well and good with your partner, and a more compelling approach to address issues in your relationship.

Exercise: What's Your Level of Self-Compassion?

Given the significance of self-compassion in reducing attachment related anxiety, you may think that it's supportive to evaluate yourself in every one of the components that make it up: self-thought, regular mankind, and mindfulness too. On a size of 1-5, rate how well you relate to the announcements in a zone. Then divide this by the quantity of proclamations in every zone to get your last appraising for the region.

Self-Kindness

_____You are tolerating and delicate with yourself in light of either your flaws or insufficiencies.

_____ You are tolerating and delicate with yourself when you commit mistakes.

_____ You are mindful and sustain yourself when you are harming or genuinely annoyed.

_____ You need to treat yourself well so you can be cheerful in the long haul.

Total: _____ ÷ _____ 4 = _____

Regular Humanity

_____ You accept others having shortcomings, flaws, or insufficiencies simply as you do.

_____ You can think about your struggles as a feature of being human; you understand that you are not the only one in them.

_____ When vexed, you can recall that, once in a while, others have comparative battles and emotions.

_____ Recollecting that others at times have comparative battles and emotions causes you to feel less alone.

Total: _____ ÷ _____ 4 = _____

Mindfulness

_____You can acknowledge your thoughts and emotions without making a decision about them—at least, whenever disturbed.

_____You can acknowledge your thoughts and feelings without denying, smothering, or misrepresenting them.

_____You can encounter your feelings without getting excessively related to them and thus losing viewpoint.

_____When vexed or during testing times, you attempt to keep up a sound viewpoint.

Total: _____ ÷ _____ 4 = _____

The higher your score for a region (the most noteworthy score being a 5), the more grounded you are in it. For any zones of shortcoming, you might decide to concentrate more on the exercises that target reinforcing them.

Advantages of Self-Compassion

Understand the advantages of self-empathy, think about this model: Dan is at a gathering with his date Jill and her friends. He doesn't think a lot about workmanship, which is the thing that the greater part of their professions or interests appear to rotate around. As opposed to chance, losing Jill's regard by saying an inappropriate thing, he absolutely closes down and doesn't let out the slightest peep. He identifies with his experience of disarray with fear of being viewed as awkward. On the other hand, Lucas—who is with his better half Sophie at the opening of a craftsmanship appear, he however thinks minimal about workmanship—isn't stressed over being seen as awkward. He acknowledges that all individuals have qualities and shortcomings. He identifies with his disarray about how to continue by recognizing his impediments. So he poses mindful inquiries, acknowledges the experiences offered, and likes the information he gains as well. As anyone might expect, Dan makes no partners among Jill's friends, who see him as far off; while Lucas enjoys a charming night with Sophie and her friends, who enjoy offering their ability to a willing and enthusiastic crowd.

Lucas, who is safely connected, has been delighted in an adolescence of feeling acknowledged and console by his folks. He took in these positive collaborations and built up a psychological portrayal of his folks (his attachment figures). This psychological portrayal normally "steps in" whenever, as a grown-up, he feels awkward or compromised in any ability, consoling him that he is a commendable individual.

133

On the other hand, Dan was raised by loving guardians, yet they couldn't reliably comfort his nerves as a kid. Well, he mainly felt upbeat in relationship until his last year of school, when he built up his first genuine attachment with Susan. She was exceptionally basic and in the end went behind his back with his friend; and afterward, she dumped him. Since that time—particularly with ladies—he would in general act naturally basic, to feel incredibly restless with ladies, and to feel especially fearful of, and helpless against, rejection. His method of adapting to this was to stay silent with the goal that he didn't uncover his insufficiencies and could ideally keep away from rejection. This regularly exploded backward because ladies felt they were not able to connect with him.

If—like Dan—you will in general uncertainty your value and be critical to yourself, research in self-compassion offers you some uplifting news. There's solid proof that self-empathy is identified with the ability to see fact all the more equitably, have understanding, and be propelled to accomplish self-awareness—all of which can assist you with defeating your inclination to self-confirm your attachment related anxiety. On the side of this present, there's likewise proof that self-empathy can assist you with feeling more socially connected, increasingly happy with life, and to have a more prominent feeling of wellbeing.

Critically, with self-empathy, you feel deserving of bliss, love, and warmth significantly after disappointment, or when confronting your confinements or shortcomings. In this way, it could be said, you can't lose. You can put yourself out there, flirt with disappointment, grapple with individual evil presences, as well as keep on review yourself decidedly as somebody who is learning and developing. The outcome is a more joyful you with more prominent possibilities for a more joyful relationship. (I state more noteworthy possibilities for a more joyful relationship because, regardless of what you do, you need your partner to work with you to support a fruitful relationship.)

The Healing Power of Compassionate Self-Awareness

If you think that it's difficult to be merciful toward your own battles, then you have to create sympathetic mindfulness. Each piece of humane mindfulness gives an essential component to getting unstuck. To audit, the principle components are mindfulness and self-empathy.

Mindfulness

Familiarity with feelings

- Identification of your feelings

- Conscious experience of your feelings

Awareness of thoughts

- Objective awareness of thoughts

- Allowing yourself to perceive how you sustain your attachment related anxiety

Mentalizing

- Maintaining scholarly point of view about yourself while staying genuinely associated together with your encounters

- An intelligent position that allows you to think about potential purposes behind your feelings, thoughts, and practices, just as those of your partner

- Understanding how your method of seeing yourself and your partner may be one-sided ur accomplice may be one-sided

Self-Compassion

- Acceptance of yourself

- Compassionate reaction to your pain

Individuals high in self-empathy experience times of agony and trouble simply like any other person. They need assistance from others; they need association, backing, and exhortation. In any case, they have a few unmistakable preferences. They are more tolerating of themselves; they are better at sustaining solid relationships; they can use proper counsel or input when they commit errors or are battling with specific issues; and they are stronger.

If you don't have a lot of self-empathy, you—sadly—can't simply will it to exist. However, through humane mindfulness, you are able to create it and support a more noteworthy joy inside yourself and inside your relationship. If you are not in a relationship, it can even now assist you with feeling decidedly about yourself, just as to move toward finding a partner in a more compelling manner.

To explain how this functions, think about Peter. He is a forty-five-year-old single guy who might want to wed. When he meets Amanda, he is captivated of her and chooses to absolutely give himself to this new relationship completely. He spills himself out to her, confident that she will acknowledge and adore him. He can be so open, to some extent, since he supersedes and attempts to overlook his feelings of fear that she might dismiss him. With time, nonetheless, he knows that he's starting to feel inaccessible from her (attention to feelings). He's aware of being disparaging of her. He thinks things like, "She can be truly irritating," or "It's very little fun investing energy with her" (attention to thoughts). From the start he feels that perhaps there's sufficiently not science.

However, when she can't get along with him one night, he misses her immediately, fears she'll leave, and is anxiety to win her adoration once more (awareness of feelings and thoughts). By then, he understands (with the assistance of mentalizing) that the issue isn't an absence of science between them. He can see that he has naturally shielded himself from getting injured by being condemning of her. With this knowledge, he can see his feelings and exercises as justifiable and human (self-empathy). Therefore, as opposed to cutting off the association as he had been thinking about, he has another choice—to confront his fear of rejection. After much help and consolation from friends, he converses with her about this fear, permitting himself to be really powerless. This prompts them cooperating on building emotional closeness—an association past simply sharing the details of their lives.

Without attention to thoughts and emotions, mentalizing, and self-empathy, Peter's story probably won't have finished so well. He may have inferred that there was just no science and said a final farewell to Amanda.

Or maybe then again regardless of whether they had hitched, he would probably have swayed between being basic and far off, on one hand, and enthusiastically occupied with attempting to prevail upon her or console himself of her adoration, on the other. On the other hand, she may have felt an absence of association with him and in the long run severed the relationship. If he were as yet ignorant of his battle when she did this, he would have been left confused, as well as incapable to understand what turned out badly. And, if this was a long-standing example for him, he may then have addressed what wasn't right with him that was continually making him be dismissed.

Compassionate mindfulness is viable because it gives an approach to individuals to work with their internal clashes, as Peter did. If you are amazingly vexed about certain issues in your relationship, you or your partner requesting that you "stop stressing" won't certainly fix anything. It may even heighten your emotions—transforming them into a tidal wave that will overpower any positive exertion to address the current issues. On occasions like this, sympathetic mindfulness can push you to understand your battles and approach them in a mindful, delicate way—eventually permitting you to support the relationship you need.

I can think about not any more concise or increasingly smooth approach to depict compassionate mindfulness than this announcement (broadly credited to dramatist August Wilson): "Stand up to the dark pieces of yourself, and work to expel them with light and absolution. Your readiness to grapple with your devils will make your heavenly angels sing. Use the agony as fuel and as a token of your strength."

Chapter six: How To Develop Self-Awareness

As I've clarified, you have valid explanations for keeping up your attachment related anxiety—it can feel like a matter of endurance. If you try to lessen this anxiety, your obstruction will normally run deep. This is genuine regardless of whether you intentionally need to change and would be more beneficial for it. So if you are determined to improving your relationship, or scanning for one, approach it carefully. Anticipate that internal opposition and plan should endure. Rather than attempting to overwhelm (or menace) yourself with requests to appear as something else, try to "become friend" with your encounters. Similarly as with any new friends, you will genuinely attempt to become more acquainted with and get them. Additionally, recall that those parts of you that are clutching attachment related anxiety are attempting to defende you—so draw in with them delicately.

Start by freeing yourself up in order to evolve. Then you can proceed onward to getting more mindful and tolerating of your feelings, picking up mindfulness and viewpoint with respect to your thoughts, and expanding your ability to mentalize.

The parts underneath offer ways to create in every one of these zones. Attempt the exercises that appear to address where you have to, and are prepared to, develop. Destroy whatever request is generally supportive, and repeat practices as you see fit for you. Be aware of a powerful urge not to do an exercise or to a repugnance for pondering some specific area, could be a misinformed exertion by your unconscious to safeguard you, and might uncover a significant region that you have to take a shot at. So give genuine thought to what that area is tending to and to attempting the exercise in it.

Oppose the compulsion to "push through the book" without truly engrossing what the exercises bring to the table. Don't hesitate to take a shot at a specific exercise for some time, or even to come back to that exercise later on for reading it.

Confronting Your Ambivalence

To build up a safe romantic relationship, it assists with monitoring your inner conflict toward freeing yourself up to the powerlessness that this objective constantly brings. It's this mindfulness that can aid you with seeing when and how your attachment related anxiety keeps you from improving your relationship.

For example, Andy realized that communication is significant in relationship, so he constrained himself to converse with her, except of being removed lately. Nonetheless, because he neglected to recognize exactly how undermined he believed, he unknowingly secured himself by conveying the message in an antagonistic and accusatory way ("We should not be hitched. Truly, you're of no help to me!"). This just served to make more separation. Had he been increasingly mindful of needing to talk, yet, in addition, needing to abstain from getting injured, he would have had the chance to discuss his fear, which would have been sure to evoke a mindful reaction from his better half.

By confronting your inner conflict, you are likewise confronting your apprehensions that you are shameful of affection (or that your partner may see you along these lines), and that you may lose the relationship you need to such an extent. This is quite difficult. However, by doing it, you will see when your postponement or self-damage efforts improve your adoration life.

As you gain this mindfulness, approach your feelings of fear and anxieties carefully. Make little strides. Set yourself up for change by intentionally working with your uncertainty.

Do this in the manner it works for you, for example, giving yourself an opportunity to think about your battles, journaling, chatting with a strong friend, or communicating your battles imaginatively, maybe by painting, or composing verse.

It's essential to understand that a more noteworthy mindfulness doesn't mean you need to act any in an unexpected way. So, dismiss this weight from yourself. For example, recognizing that you feel hurt by your partner doesn't mean you should leave her. Nonetheless, when you are trapped in a terrible example, a more noteworthy mindfulness will assist you with seeing how your examples of behavior are agonizing. This builds the odds that you will need to accomplish something in an unexpected way. To this end, it may assist with conversing with somebody you trust about your issues, or to read a good self-improvement guide. At times, you may even discover motivation in a novel or film. For example, viewing the film Silver Linings Playbook (2012) might assist you with feeling that you can discover love and joy even with your enthusiastic battles.

Confronting inner conflict is something you'll have to do over and again, as you challenge yourself to turn out to be more secure and to react differently in relationship. However, at every one of these occasions, when you are prepared to make the following stride, whatever it is, get it done. Be mindful to not fall into the trap of reasoning…and reexamining… and rethink about your situation. Recollect the saying, "Make the most out of present opportunities"? Presently an ideal opportunity to apply it.

Sustaining Awareness of Emotions

Individuals experience issues recognizing their feelings for some reasons. If you experience problems with this, it might be because you are distant from them, or, on the other hand, maybe you don't have the foggiest idea about the words to best portray them. Or you may be concentrating more on your reasoning. Or on the other hand disregarding your feelings with general portrayals, for example, "upset" or "troubled."

If you have attachment related anxiety, you are probably going to find that your feelings sometimes work in force and appear to merge together, leaving you feeling overpowered by one huge, unidentifiable mass of feeling.

Essentially recognizing and marking feelings can deactivate the piece of your brain that triggers your extraordinary pain.

By finishing the following exercise, "Distinguishing Your Emotions," you can discover how to recognize and separate your feelings. In doing as such, you'll likewise decrease their power and your trouble, which will, therefore, empower you to figure out how to tolerate them better. Then you'll be in a superior situation to sustain a closer relationship by imparting them to your partner in a useful way.

In experiencing this procedure, it is significant that you build up the ability to both open up to your feelings and close yourself off to them. For instance, you can truly help yourself feel your fear of rejection, which will feel "right" in what it is your authentic experience. However, then, after some season of connecting with that experience, you may find that you are simply delving yourself more deep into a troublesome gap, or making a more prominent feeling of emotional tumult. I have found, as far as I can tell, that individuals for the most part know when they are beneficially interfacing with their feelings instead of simply making themselves increasingly annoyed.

The thought is that, similarly likewise with any new ability, you need to stay in the ill-defined situation—a little past what is agreeable, yet not so out of sight you are exceeding. While meeting your feelings gets counterproductive, it's an ideal opportunity to abandon this procedure and take part in something bettering like, lunch with a friend, watching a film, or appreciating a stroll in the recreation center.

Exercise: Identifying Your Emotions

You can discover pieces of information of your feelings in the current situation, your real sensations, and your practices. So screen these regularly. If you will in general do well with organized assistance, make an outline with a section for every one of these territories, as depicted underneath. Or, on the other hand, if you like, basically think about the regions, it can assist with doing this at specific times, for example, in the first part of the day or at suppers. You may likewise discuss them with a trusted friend or your partner.

In spite of the fact that I examined the distinction among thoughts and feelings in the last part, the partition between these two things isn't supreme. Individuals' thoughts or view of a situation regularly influence their feelings.

For instance, you may feel deeply miserable when you think about your impression of yourself as having no worth to other people. For this situation, it is better to state that you feel "useless" or "pitiful" than to mark your feeling as "tragic." Even however these words reflect thoughts or decisions, they additionally express an emotional encounter. Also, in the arouse of discovering that your life partner has had an illicit relationship, your hurt and outrage would mix in with your thoughts to leave you feeling betrayed. So as you think about your feelings, you may find that they are impacted in one way or intermixed with your thoughts.

Date: By recording the date, you can assist with following examples in your feelings, particularly if you come back to this exercise in different occasions.

Situation: Make note of every situation whre you feel anxious. For instance, you may see that your significant other isn't home for dinner for the third time this week, and that he just let you realize he'd be late.

Sensations: Pay attention regarding how you feel in your body. For example, when you discovered that your partner would have been home late, you felt tight in your chest and even built up a cerebral pain immediately after.

In different situations, you may feel hot, discombobulated, or unstable, or you may have "butterflies" in your stomach.

Practices: Note what you did in that situation. In our model, you may record that you got off the telephone rapidly and afterward cried, or tossed something.

Attentions: Note your thoughts in that situation, yours and your partner's one. In this way, in this section you may express, "It's not alright for him to continue doing this. I wonder what I'm fouling up that is driving him away. I figure he may be cheating on me."

Feelings: As you take care of your sensations, practices, and thoughts, do specific feelings arise? Instead of attempting to force a name of what you figure you "should" be feeling, try letting the names of the feelings bubble up. For example, you may express, "Dissatisfaction, outrage, anxiety, fear of rejection, hurt, disloyalty."

If this shows to be excessively difficultkeep in mind that if you feel different feeling at the same time it's normal; you can have essential feelings, (for example, happy, irate, and apprehensive); blends of feelings (amazed + dismal = baffled); and mixes of feelings and attentions (euphoric + saw achievement = pleased).

Remember that you may be encountering various feelings—even some that contention with one another.

By recognizing your feelings, you are also recognizing your experience. This is crucial in getting yourself, dealing with your feelings viably, and speaking with your partner in a way that empowers him to get you, and ideally to connect with you, as well. Along these lines, particularly if you battle with recognizing your feelings, this exercise is well worth practicing.

Enduring Your Emotions

As you open up to mindfulness, it is basic that you have the option to endure your feelings. You should have the option to persevere through emotional sadness while fighting the temptation to attempt to make it quickly vanish, which would keep you from completely connecting, understanding, and grappling with the experience. Neural pliancy, the capacity of the mind to change, is the thing that empowers this working-through procedure to help you in the long run relate diversely to your feelings. You can expand resilience of your feelings by presenting yourself to them. You can do this through care and reflection. You can likewise do it by moving toward your feelings with interest.

Since being interested about your encounters implies needing to find out about them, such interest will normally assist you with staying open to your feelings, regardless of the anxiety. This, therefore, will empower you to better investigate them and all the more completely, and to discover and coordinate importance from your recently perceived emotions. This positive center can assist you with developing a more prominent capacity to bear upsetting feelings. One approach to create interest is by essentially finishing the past exercise, "Recognizing Your

Emotions", yet with a choice to move toward it with an open and inquisitive brain.

Exercise: Befriending Your Emotions

As you build up a capacity to tolerate your feelings, you can chip away at being increasingly open to them, and eventually, become friends with them. To become a close acquaintance with your feelings is to welcome them into your life, since you see a value in them. No, you wouldn't effectively need to feel upset; however, you could be appreciative for the advantages that a specific situation and its related feelings bring to your life.

For example, you may value your depression since it rouses you to get going on trying to meet new individuals.

You can start the procedure by contemplating explicit emotional situations and thinking about the addition:

• Do your feelings assist you with understanding the situation or your collaboration better?

• Are your feelings a warning that there is a problem you have to take care of?

• Are your feelings a declaration of compassion, helping you connect with your partner or others?

Through these inquiries you can move closer toward your feelings as you would with a friend, with an open heart. It assists with recollecting that feelings are part of a being human, at least, when they are difficult. It likewise assists with showing restraint toward yourself; figuring out how to become friends with your feelings can be a drawn out venture and an aptitude that you should rehearse for an incredible rest.

Changing Your Thoughts with Greater Awareness

As clarified in the last section, your thoughts impact you on several levels. If you focus on, and increment your familiarity with, your attachment related anxiety attentions and their belongings, you may start to address them. At times, you can basically substitute new, more beneficial speculation for the previous, reckless thoughts.

For example, you may decide to concentrate on your habit to repeat, "I haven't had a sweetheart in so long; I'm such a failure." You can start by monitoring each time you express this to yourself, and afterward supplant that idea with a more positive message: "I've had a drought for some time, however I've been in relationship previously and I can discover somebody uncommon once again." If you accept this new message by any means, you might think it consequently by deliberately practicing it.

Try not to be no picnic for yourself if this doesn't work. The methodology has its cutoff points. If the new explanation is in direct clash with your self-discernments, repeating it will never be completely persuading, likewise as you will never persuade yourself that night is day, regardless of how frequently you mark the moon as the sun.

What's most significant at this point, is that you become increasingly mindful of your thoughts and how they influence you. By doing this, you are setting up a strong establishment for understanding your feelings and convictions about yourself and your relationships, and for relating contrastingly to those emotions as well as convictions. For example, again think about consciousness of having the regular idea, "I haven't had a sweetheart in so long; I'm such a washout." You may likewise come to understand that each time you have that contemplation, maybe you are giving yourself an infusion of both gloom and sadness. When you understand this, you have a superior understanding of how your feelings work. Making this association, is a significant step in relating more decidedly to yourself.

Exercise: Changing Your "Thought Bubble"

Your negative thoughts—either as self-reactions or as recognitions that your partner doesn't adequately esteem you—sustain your attachment related anxiety. In order to straightforwardly change these thoughts, or if nothing else reduce their impact on you, complete the outline on the accompanying page.

As with so much else I've tended to, it's critical to show restraint toward yourself. You are attempting to change a method of being that has most likely been with you since adolescence, so it will take some effort in order to set up another perspective and feeling. Invest some energy looking into the diagram. Diary about it. Talk with a steady friend. Think about it until you understand how your reasoning has recently messed up yourself and your relationships—and until you are aware of when and how your reasoning is at present making issues for yourself.

To start with, make a diagram that you can fill in every day. Name five sections: Date, Situation, Attachment-Related Anxious Thoughts (identified with your partner and you), Effects of Thoughts on Feelings and Behaviors, and Disconfirming Evidence.

Date: Noting the date will definitely assist you with monitoring patterns, particularly if you complete this during various timeframes.

Situation: Write down insights concerning the situation identified with your current, past, or potential partner that activated you to get irritated. For instance, you may be vexed when your beau goes out with the folks.

Attachment Related Anxious Thoughts: Ask yourself, "What thoughts fortify my attachment related anxiety?" It can be useful to note thoughts related both to yourself and to your partner. Here are a few models:

• If I was more fascinating, he'd feel more grounded about our relationship and invest energy with me rather than the folks.

• If I would be prettier, he should stay with me.

• He'll leave once he truly becomes more acquainted with me, or once he discovers somebody better.

• He wouldn't like to spend time with me, so there must be some kind of problem with me.

• He couldn't care less how I feel.

Impacts of Thoughts on Feelings and Behaviors: Once you are clear about what you state to yourself, think about how this affects you, and how it impacts your practices. For instance, if you are continually pondering how your sweetheart is going to leave you, you will most likely feel anxiety and effectively activated envy, and may act possessively.

This is a hopeless scenario. If he truly is focused on the relationship, you won't see this and will be troubled. If he isn't submitted, you might in any case stick to the relationship, staying drenched in an urgent need to demonstrate your worth to him.

Disconfirming Evidence: Pay thoughtfulness regarding how your responses unfurl in day by day life and how they are an outcome of your imperfect intuition instead of the probable truth of your condition. Your habit to self-confirm attachment related anxiety can make this a dubious appraisal. In any case, try debating for the sake of debating with yourself. For instance, if you stress that your beau's going out with the folks implies he's not intrigued by you, you should seriously think about these inquiries:

• What proof is there for the possibility that he may be content with me? (For example, he told me he loves me; he messages or think about me consistently; he dealt with me when I was wiped out.)

• how am I incredulous of myself? (For example, I see myself as exhausting or moronic for intuition he'd need a future with me.)

• If my closest friend were in a similar situation, would I contemplate her and her situation? If not, what might I think? (For example, I'd thoroughly think about his needing to go with the folks has nothing to do at all with how intriguing she is. He gives her that he wants to think about it, so plainly he really needs to be with her.)

What you are searching for is, as is commonly said in court, "a sad remnant of an uncertainty" for you to use as an explanation behind thinking about different perspectives regarding both yourself and your partner. If there is no reasonable shadow of an uncertainty about your negative view of your partner, it might be an ideal opportunity to address them with him—or to proceed onward. If you can't make a move in both of these ways, or if you have no practical uncertainty about your negative self-observations, you will definitely profit by adding self-empathy to your creating mindfulness. If that is the situation, you may just proceed onward to the following area.

If the disconfirming proof imparts some genuine uncertainty and the acknowledgment of the negative impacts of your reasoning, you might normally build up a more positive point of view as you keep on rounding out the outline.

You can assist this with handling along by effectively helping yourself to remember the disconfirming proof whenever you know about mounting attachment related anxiety. Decide to concentrate on the more positive and sensible methods of seeing your situation. For example, when you feel anxiety about your beau leaving, you may take note of the fact that he messages you day by day and appears to be glad to see you when you go out together.

If your attachment related anxiety thoughts stay settled in, or change is by all accounts coming too gradually, you may require somewhat more assistance. You can discover this assistance by effectively building up your ability for self-empathy.

Mentalizing

Mentalizing includes a lucidity of both heart and brain. It's a sincerely associated, scholarly understanding of why you and your partner feel and go about as you do. With it, you can turn around your standard conceited discernments by observing yourself well as well as understanding your partner from within.

More explicitly, it furnishes you with knowledge that encourages you to understand:

- The reasons for trouble

- The effect of experiencing childhood in your "group of birthplace" (your mom, father, kin) on your relationship

- The effect of different encounters on your relationship

- The impediments to a more beneficial and increasingly personal attachment

- The reasons you become irrationally furious about occasions.

Remember that your attachment related anxiety is related with your impulse to endure. Along these lines, given its significance, it can a few times overpower you and make mentalizing quite difficult. Nonetheless, you can access experiences about your psychological states, or those of your partner, by thinking about thoughts, feelings, and practices as well. For example, you may be warned to your degree of outrage with your partner by your unconstrained upheaval or your dream of hitting her.

You can also improve your mentalizing by deliberately "playing" with various thoughts, creating tales concerning why you are feeling and acting some specific way, or why your partner is doing so. Criticism from your partner or believed others can help in this procedure. Yet, picking up this sort of viewpoint isn't simple, along these lines, once more, show restraint. Anticipate that it should require some investment and exertion. If it's simply excessively hard, think about seeing an advisor who is able to support you.

Exercise: Choose to Be Curious

Perhaps the most ideal ways to fortify your capacity to mentalize is to deliberately turn out to be more inquisitive about yourself or your partner. In this exercise, you will concentrate on creating various methods of survey your partner. Significantly, the objective is to think about different perspectives, not simply to locate the "right" one. This will surely assist you with developing a style of staying open to conceivable outcomes as opposed to immediately clasping down on them with one judgment, similar to a steel trap.

Do this by following these four stages:

1. Pick a situation. Pick some conduct or cooperation—positive or negative—to concentrate on whatever you have inquiries concerning, or that you could not be right about.

Model: Sybil's neighbor Russ welcomed her out on the town. Since she battles with low confidence and because he realized she hadn't gone out with anybody in some time, she calculated that it was a "feel sorry for date."

2. Check in with what you are both feeling and thinking. Make an exhaustive showing of this—you may even need to counsel the "Recognizing Your Emotions" practice prior in this part.

Model: Sybil may initially know about inclination unreliable, confused, apprehensive, and restless. Then she may understand that, regardless of herself, she was energized, felt needed, was pulled in to Russ, and was interested by the chance of a relationship. She may also understand that she was incredulous of herself—thinking she was an imbecile and feeling irate that she had gotten her expectations up.

3. Think about potential clarifications. Whenever you can associate with and distinguish your feelings and thoughts, think

about the potential reasons why the episode occurred, using what you think about yourself and your partner as well.

Model: Sybil may imagine that Russ potentially asked her out because he was exhausted, because he felt sorry for her, since he needed to simply be going out as friends, or—possibly—because he preferred her.

4. Discover fact. For the reasons for this exercise, this last step isn't really significant—that is, what's fundamental here isn't that you surmise effectively about the inspirations of your partner. Rather, the reason for this exercise is to free yourself up to think about potential outcomes as you stay associated with however you feel. Well, when you are increasingly open, you may discover an answer that is upheld by the proof around you and that reverberates inside you as exact, regardless of whether it isn't happy.

Model: While Sybil may decide not to ask Russ through and through for what valid reason he asked her out—in spite of truly needing to—she could search for indications of his aims.

For instance, it would mean a certain something if he referenced that his different friends were all away this weekend, however very another if he admitted that he discovered her appealing and needed to approach her out for quite a while.

Note: The models in this exercise concentrated on attempting to understand another person. However, you can likewise finish this exercise by concentrating on yourself. As I've noted, we can be oblivious to our own expectations as well as battles.

Exercise: Getting to Know Your Partner from the Inside Out

Mentalizing can assist you with becoming genuinely closer to your partner since it can give you a window into her fact. It does this by giving you a more itemized understanding of her experience.

You will likely truly observe the world through your partner's eyes, including what she watched, felt, and thought as well. Remember that you don't need to concur. Likewise, you don't need a grainy home-film to see, yet rather to a greater degree a top notch, being-from her-perspective experience.

Remember the accompanying when your partner is conversing with you about an encounter (it could be anything from going fishing to grieving the demise of a parent).

DO:

• Give her everything of your attention—no performing various tasks.

• Tell your partner you're keen on catching wind of the point.

- At suitable occasions, request more detail or clarification so you can truly "get it"— the facts and her thoughts as well as her emotions.

- Note nonverbal signals for a superior feeling of the power and nature of her experience.

- Be available to her point of view, especially when it doesn't coordinate yours.

DON'T:

- Multitask—not even to simply look at that approaching content.

- Interrupt, only if you are confused and need explanation.

- Assume you recognize what she is thinking or feeling.

- Try to tackle an issue (except if you are asked to).

- Tell her she's off-base about the facts or her experience.

With time, your efforts will pay off. You will feel closer to your partner and she will feel closer to you. This will likewise go far toward easing any pointless feelings of fear of rejection.

Last Thoughts on Self-Awareness

Mindfulness requires persistence. It must happen at an ideal degree of strain between recently creating mindfulness and old impression of both yourself and your partner. Something else, self-check will supersede your new mindfulness, regardless of whether it be thoughts, feelings, or mentalizing.

Along these lines, help yourself to remember this. Think, on a daily basis, to complete the exercises in this book, talk with your partner, and offer with other confided in loved ones. Most importantly, continue with your investigation of better ways of connecting with your own understanding as well as with your partner.

Manufactured by Amazon.ca
Acheson, AB